One reason that open-fire cooking still flourishes is that it is so flexible – the development of new techniques is going on all the time. Indeed, braai competitions, where innovative ideas are demonstrated in practice, have shown that in braaiing few 'rules', as such, apply. Guidelines can be given to beginners but essentially braaiing is a personal skill, one acquired by experience and developed to suit the individual's taste and lifestyle.

Much of the appeal of the braai lies in its blend of earthy simplicity and more sophisticated culinary art. This book is a guide to achieving such a blend and contains an exciting variety of recipes, tips and ideas for both the novice and the expert.

TIME FOR RELAXING

More than anything else a braai is an easy and informal way of entertaining, whether your guests are 'just a few friends' or a crowd of 20 or more. In the open air the smoky aroma of outdoor cooking and the anticipation of a veritable feast encourage relaxation in hosts as well as guests. In order to achieve this happy state the hosts have to plan carefully and do much of the preparation in advance. When planning a braai remember three golden rules of a successful occasion: the meal should be easy to do, easy to eat and easy to clear away.

Easy to do – the secret is thorough preparation. The braai chef should have all the necessary ingredients and utensils at his fingertips: the meat ready to go over the fire, basting mixture and condiments within reach, and tongs ready for action.

Easy to eat – have enough table space on which to put salads, breads, snacks and drinks, as well as the cooked food, and set them all out attractively. Serve foods that can be eaten with fingers or at most a fork, and in easily manageable portions. Although guests often like to wander around and socialise as they eat, provide comfortable seating and trays or small tables for those who like to stay in one place.

Easy to clear away – keep cutlery and plates to a minimum and use the disposable kind wherever possible. Wooden platters or paper plates with a separate basket base are ideal. Plastic-ware is also useful, being both durable and easily cleaned. Plastic cutlery can either be thrown away or wiped with a damp cloth. Paper cups are also a boon, but keep them filled on a windy day!

Relaxing around a built-in braai

INTRODUCTION

Smoke wisping from an open fire, the aroma of food cooking in fresh air, a convivial atmosphere – it is hardly surprising that braaiing, one of the oldest activities known to man, has survived for thousands of years. Since cave-dwelling times the practice has been experimented with and refined by cultures throughout the world and today South Africans are as familiar with the Japanese hibachi, the American Weber, the Argentinian asado and the Middle Eastern kebab as they are with their own potjiekos.

Part of the success of the occasion will rest in the atmosphere created. In the evening lamps or candles produce a friendly glow or, for smaller groups, the fire itself provides a focus of cosiness. If you are entertaining a crowd of people who don't know each other very well, try organising a fondue or stir-fry braai. As they cook their own selection of food and experiment with sauces, the ice will soon be broken.

The beauty of a braai is that the host, or hostess, at the fire is the centre of attention and if he is so inclined, he can do some 'real' entertaining by, for instance, flaming a whole fillet in front of the guests, carving it deftly and setting the slices out neatly on a wooden platter. Practice may be required but once perfected, the display is bound to impress.

Safety first

Make sure the braai remains a happy occasion by avoiding mishaps. Site the fire away from any vegetation that may catch alight, keep it under control at all times and extinguish it properly at the end of the proceedings.

BRAAI APPARATUS

The objective of a braai is simply to apply direct and often intense heat to food until it is cooked, and the apparatus used should allow you to achieve this with as little fuss as possible. The minimum requirements are: a bed of coals to provide the heat; and a grid on which to hold the food above the coals. In addition, it must be possible to vary the distance between the grid and the coals, thus controlling the temperature at which the food cooks.

Veld braai

The most elementary form of open-fire cooking, the veld braai, takes place over a fire surrounded by a low wall of stones. As well as supporting the grid, the stones protect the fire from wind which may cause it to burn too hot, or to burn out before cooking is complete. The height of the grid above the coals can be adjusted simply by adding or removing stones.

A variation on this theme – and there are many if you are prepared to improvise – is the 'oil-drum braai'. The sides of an oil drum cut in half lengthwise protect the fire from wind, while bricks placed inside the drum form an adjustable rest for the grid.

Built-in braai

At the other extreme, a built-in braai area on the patio or in the garden is a feature of many homes and an integral part of the outdoor lifestyle. If you intend building a braai area at home, give some thought to its siting and construction and:

● choose a sheltered spot and locate the fireplace so that the prevailing wind will blow the smoke away from the seating area
● make sure there is enough space around the fireplace for the braaier to work in peace and yet allow the guests to mingle happily
● build the fireplace at about waist height so that the base on which the coals lie is high enough to allow you to stand and braai in comfort
● allow at least two levels above the coals at which the grid can be rested so that the distance of the grid from the coals can be varied

● have a good working space immediately around the fire for plates, equipment, seasonings and bastes. You can even make it large enough to serve as a bar as well as a braai
● have a large enough serving area conveniently close to the fire
● site the braai so that in the evening it can be reached by electric light. Although a cosier atmosphere can be achieved in the dining area by candles or paraffin lamps, the braai chef will need stronger light to check the food
● place the braai within reasonable access of the kitchen

A warming oven underneath the fireplace is a useful addition, but is not essential. Similarly, space under the working surface can be used for storing wood. Some built-in braai areas include such luxuries as a smoking oven or a pizza oven.

All the ingredients for a mouth-watering braai

ROYAL BOROUGH OF GREENWICH

Follow us on twitter @greenwichlibs

P

ACKNOWLEDGEMENTS

There are a number of people whom I would like to thank for the contributions they have made to putting this book together: my fellow home economists at the Meat Board – Myrna, Hannelie, Deona, Elmarié and Saar – for compiling parts of the text, helping with the preparation for photography, and for their friendly cooperation and moral support; Sannie Smit for checking recipes and assisting with styling for the photographs – the time she spent on both tasks and the fact that she made her home available for photography are sincerely appreciated; Willie van Heerden for his enthusiastic desire to make each photograph special and for his dedication and patience; Peter Veldsman, Johan Hofmeyr and Annatjie Melck for their valuable contributions to the chapter on fish; James Forsyth for his constructive comments and sound advice on the practical aspects of braaiing; Leni Martin, the editor, for her preciseness and devotion to the book; and finally, Pieter Struik for the opportunity afforded me in bringing this book into existence.

CHRISTA KIRSTEIN
PRETORIA, 1986

Struik Lifestyle
(an imprint of Random House Struik (Pty) Ltd)
Company Reg. No. 1966/003153/07
Wembley Square, Solan Road, Gardens, Cape Town, 8001
PO Box 1144, Cape Town, 8000, South Africa

www.randomstruik.co.za

First published in 1986 by C. Struik (Pty) Ltd
Reprinted in 1987 (thrice), 1988
Second edition published in 1989 by
Struikhof Publishers (Pty) Ltd
Third edition published in 1991 by
Struik Timmins Publishers (Pty) Ltd
Fourth edition published in 1993 by Struik Publishers
Reprinted in 1994, 1995, 1997, 1998, 2000, 2001,
2002, 2004, 2005 (twice), 2006, 2007, 2008
Reprinted by Struik Lifestyle in 2009, 2010, 2012, 2013

Publisher: Linda de Villiers
Designer: Dick Ward
Illustrator: Nicci Page
Cover photographer: Malcolm Dare
Reproduction: Unifoto (Pty) Ltd, Cape Town
Printing and binding: Tien Wah Press (Pte) Ltd, Singapore

ISBN 978-1-86825-403-3

PUBLISHER'S NOTE:

Although metrication has been in use in South Africa for several years, many people are more familiar with cups and spoons than they are with millilitres. Braaiing is less exact an art than kitchen cookery and it is felt that in a book of this nature it would be helpful to the braaier to give both forms of measurement. Thus the **approximate** cup or spoon equivalent is given in brackets after the metric measurement, based on the following:

1 teaspoon	= 5 mℓ
1 tablespoon	= 15 mℓ
1 cup	= 250 mℓ

For small quantities, we believe a braaier would find it more practical to add a pinch (= 2-3 mℓ) or a dash (= 1 mℓ) of the appropriate ingredient.

CONTENTS

COMMERCIAL PORTABLE GRILLS

1 'Braai pack' – small aluminium container generally used by campers and hikers. A commercial variation of the 'veld braai', the unit is supplied complete with charcoal. Designed to be disposable.

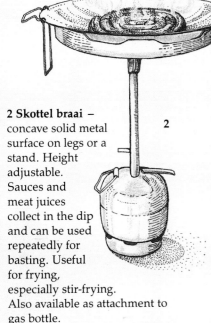

2 Skottel braai – concave solid metal surface on legs or a stand. Height adjustable. Sauces and meat juices collect in the dip and can be used repeatedly for basting. Useful for frying, especially stir-frying. Also available as attachment to gas bottle.

3 Hibachi – cast-iron container for coals. Dampers control air flow to the coals and therefore the temperature of the fire. Grid supports allow the grid to be adjusted to several different heights. Either table-top model or on a stand.

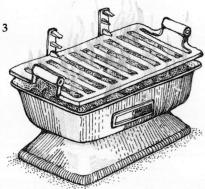

4 Gas or electric grill – produces heat for cooking by gas or electricity and is therefore much quicker and cleaner to use than wood- or charcoal-fuelled braais. This grill heats up quickly and is ready for cooking within a few minutes. Is also flexible in less-than-perfect weather conditions and can be used on a stoep or in the garage, as long as there is plenty of ventilation.

5 Open brazier – most common type, available with several optional extras. Container for coals on which grid rests. Usually on wheels for maximum mobility – should the weather turn nasty it can be moved under shelter, even in mid-braai. Grid can be placed at different heights. Extras are a movable half-cover that protects the coals from the wind, and an adjustable spit attachment.

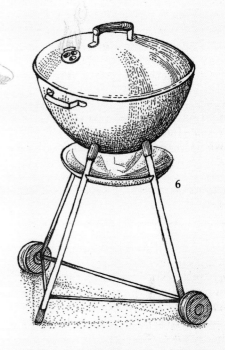

6 Covered grill or 'kettle' – has a hood or dome that reflects the heat so the meat is cooked on all sides at once and the cooking time is shortened. Particularly useful for larger cuts of meat and whole chickens. Has a large fire bowl in which a deep bed of coals can be laid. The temperature under the hood is regulated by dampers which control the air flow to the coals.

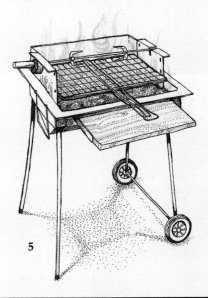

SMOKING FOODS

The idea of smoking foods under cover is that while the heat from the coals cooks the food, smoke produced by dampened wood chips or herbs on the coals gives additional flavour. Hickory or oak chips or special packs of wood chips for smoking can be bought at most camping and sports shops.

A covered grill or 'kettle' or a special smoker is usually used, but an improvised smoker comprising an oil drum and sacks also gives good results (see sketch below). The food should cook slowly in the built-up heat inside the kettle or smoker, so make sure it is not too close to the coals. In either an improvised or a commercial version, light the charcoal and let it burn until the entire surface is covered with light grey ash. Meanwhile, soak the wood chips in cold water for about 30 minutes, drain well, and when the coals are ready sprinkle the chips over them. Place the meat on the grid and close the lid.

Large joints of meat and whole chickens should be smoked over water. Light the coals and soak the wood chips in the same way as for 'dry' smoking. When the coals are ready move them to one side and place a foil dish of water under the grid. Scatter the chips over the coals, place the meat on the grid and close the lid. For both types of smoking, check from time to time that there is sufficient hot charcoal, damp chips and water.

Introduce additional flavour by scattering fresh herbs or garlic cloves on the fire, at regular intervals for large pieces of meat, and towards the end of the cooking time for fish, smaller pieces of meat and chicken

Oil-drum smoker

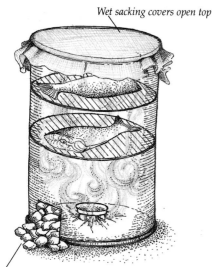

Wet sacking covers open top

Stones close hole through which fire is lit

portions. Alternatively, add wine or fruit juices to the water in the pan.

Beef, pork, venison fillet (especially kudu), fish, chicken, turkey and sausages such as frankfurters are all delicious when smoked.

BRAAI UTENSILS

The most important thing about braai utensils is to have those you will need on hand before you begin. Finding that you have to run to the kitchen for tongs just as the steak is ready to be turned results in overdone steak – or burnt fingers!

Grid – the essential item, of which, ideally, you should have two. A flat grid is used for most types of food and has the advantage that it allows you to give attention to individual pieces. A hinged grid makes turning easier when you are braaiing fragile food such as fish, or many pieces that don't need individual attention. However, if too much brute force is used in holding the two sections together, the juices are squeezed out of the meat. A reasonable compromise is a basket-type grid which supports rather than clamps the food. A fish-shaped basket can be used for braaiing whole fish.

Wire brush – should be used to clean the grid before (even if it is a new one) and after use. Get into the habit of cleaning the grid by holding it over the coals and brushing it well to remove all the ash and charred, left-on food particles.

Oven gloves – are essential for handling a hot grid, foil or even coals.

Flameproof apron – is handy to protect your clothes from flying sparks, errant flames or ash. A pocket in the apron makes a convenient holder, particularly for small items that are likely to get lost.

Tongs – long metal ones with wooden handles are necessary for turning meat. Have another pair, preferably of the scissor type, for moving coals. A fork should not be allowed anywhere near meat – the prongs damage the meat fibre and valuable juices are lost, making the meat tough.

Basting brush – again long-handled ones are best. Avoid nylon-bristled brushes as the bristles will melt if they come into contact with the grid or hot coals. A new paint brush kept specifically for basting makes a good substitute.

Spoon – also long-handled and preferably wooden, can be used for stirring sauces and spooning marinade over the meat. For potjiekos cooking, especially long-handled wooden spoons (60 - 80 cm long) can be obtained.

Sharp carving knife – is sometimes necessary to trim the meat while you are braaiing, or to carve the meat when it is ready. It is useful to have a wooden chopping board handy too, for both carving and serving.

Skewers – preferably wooden, are essential for sosaties and kebabs. As metal is a good conductor of heat, the meat immediately around a metal skewer can become overcooked. Skewers with handles make it easier to turn sosaties and kebabs.

Container of salt – keep near at hand to scatter salt on sudden flare-ups and thus douse the flames. By quenching the flames with water you will succeed only in covering the food with ash and destroying the coals. Instead of using salt, remove the food from the grid and allow the dripping fat that caused the flare-up to burn away.

Container of water – to quench the coals after the braai. If they are extinguished before they have burnt out they can be allowed to dry and then used for the next braai – resulting in quite a saving if you use charcoal briquets.

Foil – is always useful at a braai. It protects thinner areas of a piece of meat from burning while the thicker area is still cooking (such as the ribs of a lamb on the spit while the legs are still being done). It is also the wrapping (shiny side in) for meat, chicken, fish or vegetables cooked in a packet on the grid or directly among the coals. Use the heavy-duty foil rather than the thinner kind.

Meat thermometer – is useful to register the internal temperature of a large cut or meat on the spit to assess whether it is ready.

Large platters – on which to place the food before serving.

THE FIRE

Whether a braai is a dazzling success or a dismal failure depends very much on the central element, the fire, and the braaier's ability to control it.

Fuel

Wood is used by many people in preference to charcoal because wood smoke imparts a more distinctive flavour to the food. It is important to use dry or 'well-seasoned' wood as it produces better coals more quickly than 'green' wood does, and gives off very little smoke. Buy or collect wood when it is available (and usually still green) and store it until it is dry enough to use. The table below shows various kinds of wood that are available in quantity in different parts of the country and the degree of heat each kind produces.

	Cape	Transvaal	OFS	Natal	
Leadwood		x			Hot
Karee	x	x	x		Hot
Ironwood		x			Hot
Sweet thorn	x	x	x	x	Moderate - hot
Umbrella thorn		x	x	x	Moderate - hot
Hook thorn		x		x	Moderate - hot
Rooikrans	x				Moderate - hot
Vine stumps	x				Moderate

Among other woods that make excellent braai fuel, those of fruit trees such as fig and plum are favourites as they produce very good coals.

Never use:
- tamboti or oleander woods as both are poisonous
- pine or the wood of certain types of gum. The smoke from these gives food an unpleasant resinous flavour
- wood that has been painted, sealed or treated with any chemical

Charcoal is a fuel particularly popular with town-dwellers because it is readily available and is easy to use with minimum waste. Of the two kinds available – natural and briquets – the briquets give more even heat distribution over a longer time.

Where they are available, dry mealie cobs make excellent fuel. Dry pine cones are useful to start a fire – they burn readily, but they quickly disintegrate into a heap of ash.

Whatever kind of fuel you use, be generous with the amount (about 50 charcoal briquets are enough for 6 portions of meat). Don't hesitate to start a large fire and, if you intend braaiing several courses, get a second fire going to keep the first supplied with extra coals.

Starting the fire

The most important aspect of starting a fire is to light it in good time, bearing in mind that it will take 30 minutes to an hour, or even longer, depending on the type of fuel used, before the coals are ready for cooking.

There are several different ways to start a fire and everyone has his favourite, but the basics are the same. To get a wood fire going, place crumpled paper in the fireplace and add dry kindling or pine cones. Light the paper and, once the kindling is burning well, pile larger pieces of wood on top. A similar method is used for charcoal – build a pyramid of charcoal instead of kindling around the crumpled paper and when it is burning well, add more.

Commercial starters, either solid or liquid, may be used to get the fire going more quickly, but let them burn away before placing the grid over the fire as their pungent smoke will taint it. Petrol, methylated spirits or any other flammable liquid should never be poured onto a fire.

A deep and a shallow bed of coals, separated by a movable row of bricks

The shape of the fire

The shape of the fire you build depends on what you intend to braai. A solid bed of coals about 100 mm deep gives the intense heat necessary for steaks. A shallower bed about 50 mm deep provides uniform heat suitable for braaiing most other foods. The coals should extend a few centimetres beyond the area of meat on the grid. If you want to braai steaks and other foods at the same time, and the fireplace is large enough, you can arrange a large fire so that one section is twice as deep as the other. Once the steaks are done, coals from the deep fire can be used to supplement the shallower one.

A divided bed is used for large cuts of meat and spit-roasts so that heat is not concentrated directly on one small area. Position the coals on either side of or around a metal or foil drip pan and place the meat above the pan. Fat can then drip into the pan instead of splashing onto the coals and causing flare-ups and, together with the meat juices that collect in the pan, can be used for basting. Check the temperature of the coals from time to time and add extra if necessary. However, large joints should cook slowly enough that the inside cooks as well as the outside, rather than remaining raw while the outside burns. If spit-roasted meat appears to be cooking too quickly, remove the coals on one side of the pan.

Few coals, providing very low heat, are required for potjiekos. Keep the temperature constant by protecting the coals from wind (which causes them to flare and burn too hot) and by adding coals from a second fire from time to time.

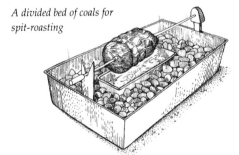

A divided bed of coals for spit-roasting

Readiness of the fire

Judging when the fire is ready for cooking is one of the first tests of a skilled braaier. A wood fire should be a mass of glowing coals that show no flame. Depending on the size of the fire, it can take an hour or more to reach this stage. The coals of a charcoal fire are ready when they look grey and ashy by day or when they glow red at night, and they reach this stage after 30 - 45 minutes. As the temperature required depends on the type of meat to be cooked, it is important to estimate the heat of the fire before putting the meat onto the grid.

Hot coals – have an ashy colour. The hand can be held 100 mm above the coals for 2 - 3 seconds.
Moderate coals – are entirely covered with grey ash, and the hand can be held 100 mm above the coals for 3 - 4 seconds.
Low coals – are covered with a thick layer of grey ash. The hand can be held 100 mm above the coals for 4 - 5 seconds.

Temperature control

Once the coals are established and the food is on the grid, there are several ways to adjust the temperature at which the food cooks:
• alter the distance between the grid and the fire – the closer the food to the coals, the higher the temperature at which it cooks
• remove some coals or add more from your second fire
• open or close the dampers of a commercial grill to increase or reduce temperature

BRAAIING MEAT

Buy quality meat

When buying meat to braai, the simple rule is: the better the meat, the better the braai. Less tender cuts should be used only for potjiekos.

Choose meat from a young, well-fed animal. According to the Meat Board grading system the following grades give the best results:
BEEF: Super A and A1
LAMB: Super Lamb and Lamb 1
PORK: Super, Grade 1 and Grade 2

If the meat is not graded, look for the following indications of quality:
COLOUR – Beef: cherry red
              Lamb: bright pink
              Pork: greyish pink
TEXTURE – the meat should be firm, smooth and silky.

FAT – should be firm, white and evenly distributed across the carcase. An oily appearance is a sign of an older animal.
CARTILAGE – should be white, soft and elastic.
RIB BONES – red spots on the surface are a sign of a young animal.
BONES – sawn bone surfaces should be red and porous.
WHITE CONNECTIVE TISSUE (sinew) – there should be very little white connective tissue.

Ripening tenderises meat

Even if the meat you intend to braai is good quality, it is likely to be tough if it hasn't been ripened or matured adequately. Ripening is a natural process which tenderises beef and lamb (pork is tender enough) and can take place either in the butcher's cool room or at home. When buying ripened meat in bulk from the butcher, order it a week in advance to allow him time to ripen it. If you prefer to ripen it yourself at home, use large, solid meat cuts with a good layer of fat to prevent the meat from drying out (steaks and chops are unsuitable for ripening once they have been cut from the carcase as they tend to dry out). Wipe the meat with a cloth wrung out in vinegar to remove bone dust and retard bacterial growth, then place the meat, uncovered, on the refrigerator shelf to allow good circulation of air around each piece. Leave beef to ripen in the refrigerator for 7 - 10 days and lamb for 2 - 5 days. The outer surface of the meat will dry out slightly and

become darker in colour. This surface layer can be trimmed away to reveal the bright red colour.

Once meat has been frozen it can no longer be ripened as the enzymatic process has been stopped.

Preparing the meat for the braai

• the thicker the raw steak, the juicier the braaied one, so buy or cut steaks no thinner than 25 mm and chops at least 20 mm thick. A cut, particularly fillet or rump, that is braaied whole and then sliced gives an even more succulent result
• scrape all bone dust from the meat surface with the back of a knife
• wipe the meat with a clean cloth moistened with vinegar
• cut off surplus fat that would drip onto the coals and cause flames to flare
• remove the rind from pork if a marinade or baste is to be used, as liquid will make the rind tough rather than crisp. The rind can be braaied separately to make crackling
• slash fat edges at 25 mm intervals to prevent the meat from curling during cooking. Remember to cut through the thin layer of connective tissue close to the meat as well
• wipe meat dry with paper towel
• sprinkle herbs (preferably fresh) of your choice and a few grindings of black pepper over the meat but don't be tempted to use salt at this stage – it draws the juices out of the meat and you will end up with a chop that is tough and dry. Rather season with salt towards the end of the cooking time or when the meat is ready

Rump steak on the grid

CUTS SUITABLE FOR BRAAIING

BEEF

Prime rib (1) and **wing rib (2)** – club steaks, Scotch fillet or rib-eye (without bone), 25 - 30 mm thick
Sirloin (3) – T-bone steaks cut from the part nearest the wing rib, 25 - 30 mm thick. (This steak has a distinct T-shaped bone with the fillet on one side and a larger eye muscle on the other)
– entrecôte steak, cut from the larger eye muscle of the T-bone, 25 - 30 mm thick
– porterhouse steaks, cut from the part nearest the rump, 50 mm thick (one steak serves two people)
Rump (4) – rump steaks, 25 - 30 mm thick
Fillet (5), the small eye muscle extending from the sirloin through the rump – fillet steaks, e.g. chateaubriand or tournedos, 25 - 30 mm thick

To enjoy a really succulent steak have all the above, except porterhouse, cut 25 - 30 mm thick. Porterhouse is best 50 mm thick.

Short ribs (6) , the last, triangular rib bones of the thin flank, and **flat rib (7)** are not as tender as the cuts listed above but are very tasty. They can be marinated and cut crosswise into portions.

Clockwise from top right: club steak, Scotch fillet, rump steak, fillet and T-bone steak

LAMB

Lamb chops most suitable for braaiing come from the **rib (1)**, **loin (2)** and **chump (3)** cuts of the carcase.
Thick rib (4) and **leg (5)** chops can also be braaied but are less tender.
For succulent chops, have them cut 20 - 25 mm thick.

Clockwise from top right:
thick rib, rib, loin and chump chops

As well as chops, other cuts of lamb can be braaied. Recipes for the cuts listed below can be found in the chapter on lamb (pages 22 - 29).

Saddle of lamb is the loin section which is removed before the carcase is halved and therefore contains two cuts of loin. Saddle chops are also cut from the loin before the carcase is halved and are therefore twice the size of ordinary loin chops.
Leg or shoulder can be spit-roasted whole (see recipe page 27), boned and cut open to form a butterfly leg or shoulder, or boned and rolled.
Breast should be sawn into ribbetjies before braaiing, and is good marinated.
Noisettes are taken from the rib or loin. The cut is boned, rolled and secured with string at 25 mm intervals. The roll of meat is then sliced between the pieces of string to form 'wheels'. Similar 'wheels' secured with skewers are known as saratoga chops.

Cutlets are taken from the rib and resemble rib chops, except that the back bone has been removed and the meat and thin membrane covering the tip of the bone have been cut away.

MUTTON

Less tender than lamb, mutton generally has more flavour and is excellent for potjiekos. Only well-ripened rib, loin and chump chops are suitable for braaiing on a grid.

PORK

Pork cuts are similar to those of lamb, apart from the **spareribs (6)** which are equivalent to the short ribs on a beef carcase.

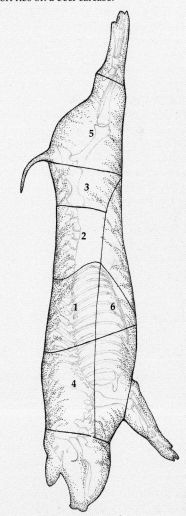

If using meat other than the cuts recommended above, the meat should be marinated, cooked in foil or braaied in a covered grill.

Preparing the grid

If you want your braai to taste like today's lamb braai and not like last week's fish braai, make sure the grid is clean. Place it over the fire to burn off any congealed fat and give it a good scrub with a wire brush. Do this to new grids, too, to remove any particles of dust or grime. Then brush cooking oil lightly over to prevent food from sticking to the grid.

When you are braaiing

• place the grid at the correct distance from the coals to achieve the required cooking temperature. A distance of 100 mm between the coals and the meat is a reasonable average if your coals are hot for steak, and moderate for chops, sausages and sosaties. If, having tested the heat of the coals by placing your hand 100 mm above them, you feel that the coals are either too hot or too cool, adjust the height of the grid, lowering it to increase the temperature at which the meat will cook, or raising it to decrease the temperature

• sear the meat quickly on each side to seal in the juices. Then turn it regularly so that it browns evenly

• apply more baste or seasonings once the meat has warmed up and 'relaxed'

• use tongs or a spatula rather than a fork to turn meat, as by piercing the meat you allow juices to escape

• season with salt while you are braaiing or just before serving

• to add atmosphere and aroma to your braai, and subtle flavour to the meat, sprinkle herbs such as rosemary or thyme, chopped onion, chives or garlic cloves on the fire. Try rosemary or mint for lamb, orange peel for pork, fennel for fish

• when sprinkling herbs directly onto the meat, use a light hand so as not to overpower the meaty flavour

Timing

The length of time it takes for the meat to be cooked to perfection depends on a number of factors: the kind of meat, the thickness of the cut, the temperature of the coals and the distance of the meat from them, what you consider to be perfection – even the prevailing weather conditions. Only approximate times can be given for when you might expect your steak or chop to be ready, and again it is the skill of the braaier to determine just when he must remove the morsel from the grid.

As a rough guide then, and taking the distance from the coals to be 100 mm:

Beef	Thickness	Cooking time
Rare	25 mm	10 - 12 minutes
Medium	25 mm	16 - 18 minutes

Lamb and pork		
Medium	20 mm	10 - 12 minutes
Well done	20 mm	14 - 16 minutes

To eat beef at its best, rare and medium are recommended, lamb is most succulent when it is medium done, and pork should be well done. Take care, however, not to overcook the meat or it will be dry and tough.

When planning a braai consider the order in which the different types of meat should be cooked. Sausages, hamburgers, chicken and spareribs can all be kept warm without spoiling so braai these first. Steaks, chops, sosaties or kebabs, and fish, however, taste better if they are served straight from the grid.

Larger cuts of meat, such as leg of lamb on the spit, cook in their latent heat even after they have been removed from the fire. Allow such cuts to 'rest' near the fire for 10 - 15 minutes while the juices are absorbed.

> To make the transport of materials easier when you are planning to braai away from home, build a fire in a cardboard box which has holes cut in the sides near the base. At the braai site you simply light the paper in the bottom of the box.

BRAAIING CHICKEN

Choosing a chicken

When buying a chicken – whether it is a 500 g baby or a 1 kg spring chicken, or in portions – there are several points to look out for:

• a plump appearance and a smooth, moist skin

• a soft, flexible and white breastbone, which identifies a young bird

• unbruised flesh, as bruising is a sign of negligent handling

• avoid chickens with an unsavoury smell

Preparing the chicken

To prepare a whole chicken for the braai, remove the giblets from the cavity and the oil gland from the tail end and check that all feathers have been stripped. Holding the bird under a tap, let cold water run through the cavity, then drain well and pat the outside dry with a clean cloth. To prepare chicken portions, remove excess fat, rinse them and pat dry.

On the braai

• braaiing a whole chicken is a long, slow process and is best done on a spit or in a covered grill. Half chickens and portions, however, can be cooked on an open grid, as can chicken kebabs, for which the breast meat is usually used. Chicken portions also make a delicious meal if they are steamed in a foil packet on the coals

• the braaiing time can be shortened if the chicken is pre-cooked. Let it simmer in a saucepan, with seasonings, for 20 minutes; oven roast it in a cooking bag at 160 °C for 20 minutes; or microwave it on full power for 8 minutes

• chicken marinates well. To let the flavour penetrate thoroughly allow 4 - 8 hours marinating time for portions, and 12 - 24 hours for a whole chicken. When marinating a whole chicken pour half the marinade into the cavity and the rest over the chicken. Turn the bird in the marinade several times

• before braaiing half a chicken break the wings so that the bird lies flat

• whole or halved chickens should be braaied with the bone side down first. The bone conducts heat, thus speeding up the cooking process, and protects the flesh from drying out

• baste the chicken regularly to add moisture and flavour, and to protect the meat from drying out over the coals

• commercial braai spices and bastes containing sugar should be used sparingly and only towards the end of the cooking time as the skin easily becomes scorched

Timing

It is difficult to suggest a specific braaiing time for chicken as whole birds as well as portions vary considerably in size. When the skin is crisp and brown, the flesh is tender, the juices run clear and, on a whole chicken, the drumstick moves freely in its socket – then the bird is cooked.

> As a general rule, the thicker the meat, the more slowly it should cook – the thinner the cut, the closer it should be to the coals.

BRAAIING FISH

Of the tremendous variety of fish caught in local waters, many are suitable for braaiing. The flesh of some, such as mackerel, sardine, tunny, yellowtail, elf and snoek, is strongly flavoured, rich and dark in colour because the oil content of the fish is distributed throughout its body. These so-called 'oily' fish can be braaied very successfully without the addition of bastes and butters, marinades and sauces, as the flesh remains moist during cooking.

In other kinds, known as 'white fish', the body oils are concentrated in the liver, leaving the flesh with a more delicate flavour and white in colour. Popular eating fish among the white fish are sole, kabeljou or cob, hake, skatewing, Hottentot, kingklip, silverfish, red roman, white steenbras and angelfish.

In general, white fish should be well basted on the braai so that they don't dry out, but some, such as angelfish and galjoen, have a fatty layer between the skin and the flesh which acts as a self-basting mechanism, ensuring that the flesh remains moist and succulent.

Choosing fish

When buying fresh fish watch out for the following characteristics:
- fresh smell
- clear eyes
- clear red gills
- firm flesh that is springy to the touch
- shiny scales that are firmly attached to the body

Bleeding a fish

The flavour of many fish, particularly galjoen, is improved if the head is cut off and the blood is allowed to drain out of the fish as soon as it has been caught.

Preparing fish

To prepare a whole fish for the braai, first slit it along the belly and clip off the gills with a sharp knife or pair of kitchen scissors. Scrape out the entrails and rinse the fish well, taking care to remove all traces of blood and the inner veins. Some people prefer to leave the skin and scales in place so that the fish is less likely to fall apart on the grid. However, if you want to scale the fish, hold it by the tail under running water and scrape off the scales with the back of a knife, working down towards the head. Do this outside if possible, or scale the fish over newspaper and then rinse it under running water.

To fillet a fish, first scale and gut it and remove the gills and fins with a pair of kitchen scissors or a sharp knife. Then, using a sharp knife, cut along the back bone from head to tail, exposing the whole bone. Starting at the tail end, cut the flesh away from the bone on one side, then turn it over and repeat on the other side. Lift out the back bone and cut the fillets away from the head. Any smaller bones left can be removed by hand or with the point of a sharp knife.

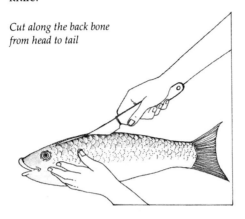

Cut along the back bone from head to tail

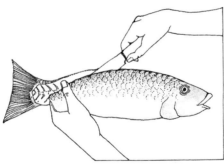

Cut the flesh away from the bone on one side, starting at the tail end

Ideally, a fish should be caught, cleaned and filleted, and put straight on the grid. If this is not possible, a cleaned fish can be kept on a bed of coarse salt in the refrigerator for three days. Fish that have been frozen and then thawed deteriorate rapidly and should be braaied within 24 hours of thawing.

On the braai

White fish should be basted well both before and during braaiing. Take care not to overpower the delicate flavour of the fish with too strong a baste – melted Lemon butter (page 89) is ideal. Because both flavour and texture are delicate, fish is delicious cooked in foil.

However, if you are braaiing the fish on a grid
- use a hinged grid or a specially designed fish 'basket' to make turning easier
- make incisions in the skin to prevent the flesh from bursting out
- give both grid and fish a light coating of oil to prevent the fish from sticking
- braai over low coals or, if the fire is moderately hot, at least 150 mm from the coals
- grill the fish skin side down first as the skin protects the flesh from the heat and stops it from drying out

'Vlekking' and salting

Some fish, particularly snoek, yellowtail, haarders and galjoen, can be 'vlekked' (cut open so that the flesh, still attached to the back bone, opens out flat), salted heavily with coarse salt and hung outside by the tail for 2 - 3 hours. This process toughens the skin so that it becomes crisp when cooked and makes the fish easier to handle on the braai. Some people prefer to wind-dry the fish without salting it.

Timing

Judge when the fish is ready by the colour of the flesh. The flesh of raw fish is watery and translucent but as the heat coagulates the protein the flesh turns a milky colour and then white. When the thickest part of the flesh is white in the middle, or when the gills can be pulled off easily, the fish is cooked through. Take care not to overcook fish as it becomes dry and tough very quickly. It should be served immediately.

As a rough guide to the cooking time, at 100 mm from the coals:

a fillet 25 mm thick	about 10 minutes
a whole fish, per 500 g	15 - 20 minutes
in foil, per 500 g	20 - 25 minutes

Have a small bowl of cooking oil and a basting brush on hand to rectify 'accidents'. If a piece of food falls on the ground or into the fire, retrieve it, hold it vertically and gently brush oil down it to remove particles of sand or ash. Then return it to the grid.

BRAAIING SHELLFISH

Crayfish (this is a popular name for the shellfish that is more correctly termed crawfish)

Like any other seafood, crayfish is best consumed fresh, and to test whether the one you have is still worth eating, stretch out its tail – if it springs back into a curled position immediately then your crayfish is fresh. A small or medium-sized specimen is best for braaiing.

Place the whole crayfish, belly downwards and tail outstretched, on a board. Using a very sharp knife and starting from the small horn between the eyes, cut through the shell right down to the last segment in the tail, which can be left intact. Open the crayfish, remove the stomach and alimentary canal, rinse and pat dry.

To braai, place the crayfish flesh down on the grid over moderate coals for 2 minutes. Turn and braai for another 15 minutes, basting frequently with melted Lemon butter (page 89). The flesh is cooked when it is opaque and pulls away easily from the shell.

Prawns and langoustines

These can be bought frozen from most supermarkets and should be thawed slowly in the refrigerator before braaiing. Once they are thawed, cut through the shell along the back and pull out the intestinal thread. Leave the shell in place, however, as it protects the flesh from the heat and prevents it from drying out. Larger prawns and langoustines can be braaied on a grid but it is easier to cook smaller prawns on a skottel braai in melted savoury butter – Lemon or Garlic butter (page 89) is recommended. The prawns or langoustines are done when the flesh is opaque.

Perlemoen

It is difficult to obtain perlemoen commercially and most people who have perlemoen to cook have a diver as a friend, or dive themselves.

To remove the flesh from the shell, insert a knife under the shell at the edge opposite the row of small holes and prise the flesh out. Using a pot scourer or stiff brush, scrub the greenish film from the flat surface, then trim off the 'skirt' and the dark area where the entrails are located. Cut the flesh horizontally into thin slices and beat them lightly with a mallet to tenderise them.

Brush the slices with melted butter and braai over hot coals for about 2 minutes on each side. Season lightly with salt and freshly ground white pepper.

Mussels

Once mussels have been gathered they must be eaten within 24 hours, and until they are cooked must be kept alive in fresh or sea water in the refrigerator. To test that they are still alive just before cooking, tap the shell firmly – if it doesn't close up immediately, throw it away. If it does close up, pull off the 'beard', scrub the shell clean and place the mussels around the edge of the grid, over low coals. When they have steamed open they are ready to eat. Serve with Garlic butter (page 89).

Alikreukels

With their shells as ready-made containers, alikreukels are very easy to braai. Simply place them open end up among moderate coals and let them cook in their own juices for about 30 minutes. They are ready when the 'trap doors' attached to the flesh can be removed easily, and the flesh can then be taken out of the shell. Cut away the dark stomach area and slice the rest. Season with salt and freshly ground white pepper, and serve with Garlic butter (page 89).

MARINADES AND BASTES

Marinades and bastes are applied to meats, poultry and fish before or in the course of braaiing for special effect. Used judiciously they add spice to the meal – used without due thought they can be disastrous.

Marinades

A marinade consists of one third cooking oil, olive oil or melted butter and two thirds acid in the form of wine, vinegar or lemon juice, or a combination thereof. To these are added the seasonings that impart the characteristic flavour to the marinade and thus to the meat. The oil prevents the meat from becoming dry and adds moisture to very lean meat such as venison. The acid of the wine, vinegar or lemon juice has a slight tenderising effect – but really tender meat can be guaranteed only if it has been well-ripened.

To achieve best results food should be marinated for 4 - 6 hours, although dry meat such as venison, tougher cuts such as chuck of beef, and special dishes such as sosaties benefit from soaking overnight or longer. Use an earthenware, ceramic, glass or plastic container for the marinade as the acid reacts with a metal surface. If the food is not completely submerged in the marinade it should be turned halfway through the marinating time.

Marinate meat in the refrigerator as, although higher temperatures may speed the marinating process, they also activate bacterial growth. The marinade can be used more than once – when the meat has been removed bring the liquid to the boil and let it cool. Alternatively, use the marinade as a baste while braaiing, and any left over can be thickened and served as a sauce with the meat.

Thickening a marinade

To thicken the marinade, heat 30 mℓ (2 tablespoons) butter and stir into it 30 mℓ (2 tablespoons) cake flour. Add 250 mℓ (1 cup) marinade and bring to the boil, stirring all the time.

Basic marinade or baste

125 mℓ (½ cup) cooking oil or olive oil
375 mℓ (1½ cups) dry red or white wine
1 clove garlic, crushed
1 small onion, sliced
freshly ground pepper to taste

Mix the ingredients thoroughly. The flavour is enhanced if the mixture is allowed to stand for a few hours.

VARIATIONS
Any number of variations can be concocted using this recipe as a base. Simply add 15 mℓ (1 tablespoon) freshly chopped or 5 mℓ (1 teaspoon) dried herbs such as:

thyme (for pork and lamb)
rosemary, oregano, marjoram (for lamb and beef)
sage or tarragon (for pork and chicken)
fennel leaves or dill (for fish)

or to create other flavours add a dash of:

mustard
soy sauce
Tabasco
Worcestershire sauce
tomato paste
chutney
honey, brown sugar or sherry
smooth apricot jam

Use a smaller quantity of the marinade mixture as a baste.

Bastes

A baste's prime function is to moisten the meat while it is being braaied, and at the same time give it a particular flavour. It is brushed onto the food with a brush or crushed herb twig (such as thyme or rosemary) and does not penetrate as deeply as the marinade.

Herb and oil baste

125 mℓ (½ cup) cooking oil or olive oil
15 mℓ (1 tablespoon) lemon juice
1 clove garlic, crushed
5 mℓ (1 teaspoon) freshly chopped or 2 mℓ (a pinch) dried rosemary
5 mℓ (1 teaspoon) freshly chopped or 2 mℓ (a pinch) dried marjoram
5 mℓ (1 teaspoon) freshly chopped or 2 mℓ (a pinch) dried parsley

Mix together all the ingredients. Using a crushed sprig of rosemary, baste the meat frequently while braaiing. This baste can be prepared in advance and kept in the refrigerator until it is needed.

> ### Sweet bastes
> If a baste contains a sweet ingredient such as fruit or fruit juice, honey, sugar, chutney, tomato sauce or jam, it will burn more easily over the fire. Turn the food more often or baste only towards the end of the cooking time.

MENUS

Today more and more people are entertaining in their own homes and a braai is an informal and pleasant way to do so. The menu need not be lavish – in fact a simple braai, well cooked and attractively served, can be just as appealing as an elaborate one. When planning a menu bear the following points in mind:

- the ideal menu should offer contrast, colour and flavour. Avoid choosing similar ingredients in different dishes and make sure that there is a variety of textures
- choose foods that are in season and likely to be at their best
- arrange the raw ingredients attractively because the meal is prepared in full view of the guests
- allow for appetites that have been sharpened by the fresh air and the smell of the food cooking – 350 - 500 g meat, fish or chicken per person
- do as much preparation as possible in advance
- plan the menu so that the dishes don't all need to be cooked on the same fire at once. If you are going to cook a dish that requires long, slow cooking (such as pap), make sure that the fire is started in good time. Before the coals are exhausted the meat and dessert must still be cooked

Raw ingredients arranged attractively

Pepper steak (back) and Cheesy mustard steaks

Cheesy mustard steaks

4 x 300 g rump steaks, 25 mm thick (club,
   T-bone or Scotch fillet can also be
   used)
30 mℓ (2 tablespoons) prepared English
   mustard
15 mℓ (1 tablespoon) cooking oil
15 mℓ (1 tablespoon) lemon juice
10 mℓ (2 teaspoons) freshly chopped
   herbs (marjoram, parsley, thyme) or
   3 mℓ (a pinch) dried mixed herbs
4 thin slices cheese (Cheddar or Gruyère)

Slash the fat edges of the steaks. Mix together the mustard, oil and lemon juice. Braai the steaks over hot coals for 5 - 6 minutes on one side, then turn and spread half the mustard mixture on the cooked side. Braai for another 5 - 6 minutes (rare) or 8 - 10 minutes (medium). Turn the steaks again and spread the remaining mustard mixture on the other side. Sprinkle with herbs and put a slice of cheese on top. Serve immediately, before the cheese starts to drip.
Serves 4

Pepper steak

4 x 300 g rump steaks, 25 mm thick
10 mℓ (2 teaspoons) cooking oil
15 mℓ (1 tablespoon) black peppercorns,
   coarsely ground
salt to taste

Slash the fat edge of each steak, brush the steak with cooking oil, then dip it in the peppercorns, coating it well. Braai the steaks over hot coals for 10 - 12 minutes (rare) or 16 - 18 minutes (medium). Season with salt and serve immediately.
Serves 4

VARIATION
The steaks can also be fried in hot cooking oil on a skottel braai.

BEEF

Tender beef, grilled to perfection, will always be food fit for a king. The secret of braaiing beef successfully is to use well-ripened meat from a young, well-fed animal. The longer beef is grilled, the more flavour and succulence it loses, so keep it rare (10 - 12 minutes) or medium (16 - 18 minutes). Make sure the coals are hot before you begin, and when the steaks are ready, serve them immediately.

Scotch fillet with braai sauce

**4 Scotch fillet steaks, 25 mm thick
   (T-bone, club or rump can also be used)**

BRAAI SAUCE
125 mℓ (½ cup) tomato sauce
60 mℓ (¼ cup) Worcestershire sauce
15 mℓ (1 tablespoon) hot chutney
5 mℓ (1 teaspoon) dry mustard
125 mℓ (½ cup) vinegar
15 mℓ (1 tablespoon) cooking oil
1 clove garlic, crushed
15 mℓ (1 tablespoon) brown sugar
125 mℓ (½ cup) cream

Slash the fat edges of the steaks. Mix together all the ingredients for the sauce, except the cream, and marinate the meat in it for about 2 hours. Remove the steaks from the sauce and braai them over hot coals for 10 - 12 minutes (rare) or 16 - 18 minutes (medium). Add the cream to the sauce, heat it slightly over the fire and serve it with the steaks.
Serves 4

VARIATION
The steaks can be braaied and served with the sauce without first being marinated.

Scotch fillet with braai sauce (back) and Club steaks in beer marinade

T-bone steak with mushroom sauce

Club steaks in beer marinade

**4 club steaks, 25 mm thick (T-bone,
   Scotch fillet or rump can also be used)**

BEER MARINADE
**250 mℓ (1 cup) Basic marinade (page 12),
   substituting beer for the wine**
5 mℓ (1 teaspoon) prepared mustard
5 mℓ (1 teaspoon) soy sauce
15 mℓ (1 tablespoon) brown sugar

Slash the fat edges of the steaks. Mix together the marinade ingredients in a saucepan and bring to the boil. Remove from the heat and cool slightly, then marinate the meat for about 2 hours. Braai the steaks over hot coals for 10 - 12 minutes (rare) or 16 - 18 minutes (medium), basting frequently with the marinade. Serve immediately.
Serves 4

T-bone steak with mushroom sauce

**6 T-bone steaks, 25 mm thick (club,
   Scotch fillet or rump can also be used)**
**60 g (¼ cup) butter, melted or 60 mℓ
   (¼ cup) Herb and oil baste (page 13)**
salt and freshly ground black pepper

MUSHROOM SAUCE
30 mℓ (2 tablespoons) butter
15 mℓ (1 tablespoon) cooking oil
300 g mushrooms, sliced
2 onions, chopped
10 mℓ (2 teaspoons) cake flour
50 mℓ (3 tablespoons) chopped parsley
30 mℓ (2 tablespoons) sherry
50 mℓ (3 tablespoons) sour cream

To make the sauce, heat the butter and cooking oil together in a saucepan or potjie, or on a skottel braai. Fry the mushrooms and onion gently until the onion is translucent, then add the cake flour and fry gently for a few minutes longer, stirring all the time. Add the parsley, sherry and sour cream just before serving. Slash the fat edges of the steaks, brush them with the melted butter or Herb and oil baste and braai them over hot coals for 10 - 12 minutes (rare) or 16 - 18 minutes (medium). Season with salt and pepper. Serve the mushroom sauce with the meat.
Serves 6

Fillet with bacon

1,5 kg whole fillet
15 mℓ (1 tablespoon) prepared mustard
6 large gherkins, chopped
freshly ground black pepper to taste
250 g rindless bacon

Make an incision lengthwise in the fillet without cutting right through. Mix together the mustard, gherkins and pepper and spread inside the meat. Close up the fillet and wrap bacon rashers around it, securing the ends with thin skewers or toothpicks. Braai over low coals for about 30 minutes (rare) or 40 minutes (medium). Remove the fillet from the fire but leave it to rest in a warm place for about 10 minutes before carving.
Serves 6

VARIATION
The fillet may be marinated in 500 mℓ (2 cups) Basic marinade (page 12) for about 5 hours before being stuffed.

---HINTS---

Fillet is a lean cut – cook it carefully so that the meat does not dry out.

Three different steaks are taken from the fillet cut. Chateaubriand, a double piece of fillet cut from the wide end at the rump, weighs about 500 g and is enough for 2 people. Tournedos steaks are cut from the thinner part of the middle section of fillet. Allow 125 g per person and cut the steaks 25 - 30 mm thick. Fillet steaks are taken from the middle part of the fillet, located in the sirloin of the carcase (see page 9). Allow 125 g per person and cut the steaks 25 - 30 mm thick.

Braai any of these steaks over hot coals for 10 - 12 minutes (rare) or 16 - 18 minutes (medium) and serve with a savoury butter or a tasty sauce.

Create a stir by flambéing a whole fillet. Braai it over moderate coals for about 25 minutes (rare) or 35 minutes (medium). When the meat is ready heat 50 mℓ (3 tablespoons) brandy in a small container over the coals, ignite it and quickly pour the flaming liquid over the meat. Then carve the fillet into thin slices across the grain.

Fillet with bacon

Entrecôte steaks with nut stuffing

4 entrecôte steaks, 25 mm thick
salt and freshly ground black pepper
to taste

NUT STUFFING
30 mℓ (2 tablespoons) chopped pecans or
walnuts
30 mℓ (2 tablespoons) cooked bone
marrow, cooled slightly
1 egg, beaten
125 mℓ (½ cup) fresh breadcrumbs

Mix together the stuffing ingredients. Cut a pocket along the length of each steak and sprinkle a little salt and pepper inside. Fill each pocket with nut stuffing and secure with a toothpick. Braai the steaks over hot coals for 10 - 12 minutes (rare) or 16 - 18 minutes (medium). Sprinkle more salt and pepper over the steaks and serve immediately.
Serves 4

VARIATION
Rice stuffing is a tasty substitute for nut stuffing. Heat 30 mℓ (2 tablespoons) cooking oil in a pan and fry 60 mℓ (¼ cup) chopped onion until it is translucent. Remove from the heat, add 125 mℓ (½ cup) cooked rice and 30 mℓ (2 tablespoons) chopped parsley, and mix well.

HINT
To cook bone marrow, boil 2 slices of beef shin in water for 15 minutes. Drain, allow to cool and remove the marrow from the centre of the bones.

Entrecôte steaks with nut stuffing

Carpetbag steaks

Carpetbag steaks

2 Scotch fillet steaks, 25 mm thick
60 g (¼ cup) Mixed herb butter (page 89)
freshly ground black pepper to taste

OYSTER STUFFING
10 mℓ (2 teaspoons) butter
1 small onion, chopped
100 g mushrooms, finely sliced (optional)
12 smoked oysters or mussels
5 mℓ (1 teaspoon) lemon juice
30 mℓ (2 tablespoons) cream
freshly ground black pepper to taste

To make the stuffing, melt the butter in a saucepan or potjie or on a skottel braai and fry the onion and mushrooms until the onion is translucent. Add the oysters, lemon juice, cream and pepper and mix lightly. Make an incision in each steak to form a pocket, fill each one with oyster stuffing and secure with toothpicks. Braai the steaks over moderate to hot coals for 10 - 12 minutes (rare) or 16 - 18 minutes (medium), then top each one with a pat of Mixed herb butter. Season with pepper and serve immediately.
Serves 2

HINT
It is easier to cut a pocket in the steak if you first place it in the freezer for about 10 minutes.

Porterhouse steak

Porterhouse steak

1 porterhouse steak, 50 mm thick

PORTERHOUSE BASTE
2 rashers rindless bacon, chopped
1 onion, chopped
1 clove garlic, crushed
75 mℓ (5 tablespoons) tomato sauce
50 mℓ (3 tablespoons) lemon juice
2 mℓ (a pinch) dry mustard
5 mℓ (1 teaspoon) salt
freshly ground black pepper to taste

To prepare the baste, fry the bacon in a heated saucepan until it is crisp. Remove the bacon and fry the onion and garlic gently in the bacon fat until the onion is translucent. Add the bacon and remaining ingredients, mix well and chill. Braai each side of the steak over moderate coals for 10 - 12 minutes (rare) or 16 - 18 minutes (medium), basting frequently. Loosen the fillet and eye muscle from the T-shaped bone and carve the meat into thin slices, following the grain. Reheat the remaining baste, pour it over the meat and serve immediately.
Serves 2

Scotch fillet on a spit

1 kg whole Scotch fillet
10 mℓ (2 teaspoons) salt
freshly ground black pepper to taste

ROSEMARY BASTE
125 mℓ (½ cup) Basic baste (page 12),
  using white wine
15 mℓ (1 tablespoon) freshly chopped or
  5 mℓ (1 teaspoon) dried rosemary

Mix together the ingredients for the baste. Thread the Scotch fillet lengthwise onto the spit and secure tightly with string. Braai the meat over moderate coals for 35 - 45 minutes, brushing frequently with the baste. Season with salt and pepper and allow the meat to rest in a warm place for 5 - 10 minutes before carving.
Serves 4

Scotch fillet on a spit

Steak wheels

3 slices rump steak, 10 mm thick (each
   about 200 g)
12 rashers rindless bacon
250 g lean beef mince
1 onion, finely chopped
1 clove garlic, finely chopped
30 mℓ (2 tablespoons) tomato paste
1 egg, beaten
15 mℓ (1 tablespoon) freshly chopped or
   5 mℓ (1 teaspoon) dried parsley
15 mℓ (1 tablespoon) freshly chopped or
   5 mℓ (1 teaspoon) dried oregano
5 mℓ (1 teaspoon) freshly chopped or 2 mℓ
   (a pinch) dried marjoram
freshly ground black pepper to taste
5 mℓ (1 teaspoon) salt

Beat the steak slices lightly with a mallet,
then place 4 bacon rashers on each slice.
Mix together the remaining ingredients.
Divide the mixture among the slices and
press it gently on the bacon to cover it. Roll
up the meat tightly, wrap it in cling wrap
and leave it in the freezer for 20 minutes.
Insert 4 skewers through each meat roll at
regular intervals and cut the meat between
the skewers. Braai the wheels over moderate coals for about 15 minutes.
Makes 12 wheels

Rump steak kebabs

600 g rump steak, cut into 25 mm cubes
6 lamb kidneys (membrane and core
   removed), halved
12 pickling onions
1 green pepper, cut into chunks
125 mℓ (½ cup) Basic baste (page 12),
   using white wine

Thread the steak cubes, kidneys, onions
and green pepper alternately onto 6 skewers. Braai the kebabs over low coals for
about 15 minutes, turning and brushing
frequently with the Basic baste. Serve
immediately.
Serves 6

Rump steak kebabs (left) and Steak wheels

Corned beef short rib with wine sauce

1 kg corned beef short rib, cut into portions

WINE SAUCE
1 onion, chopped
250 mℓ (1 cup) semi-sweet white wine
30 mℓ (2 tablespoons) tomato purée
5 mℓ (1 teaspoon) prepared mustard
125 mℓ (½ cup) cream
5 mℓ (1 teaspoon) freshly chopped or
** 2 mℓ (a pinch) dried oregano**
2 mℓ (a pinch) salt
freshly ground white pepper to taste

Cover the short rib with cold water and simmer for about 1 hour or until almost tender. Remove the meat from the liquid and pat it dry with paper towel. Braai over moderate coals for about 30 minutes. Prepare the sauce by combining the onion, wine, tomato purée and mustard in a potjie. Bring to the boil and cook for about 5 minutes. Add the cream and simmer for another 5 minutes, until the sauce has thickened. Season with the oregano, salt and pepper. Serve the sauce with the meat.
Serves 4

VARIATION
Try smoking the short rib (see page 6) instead of braaiing it over the coals.

Glazed flat rib

1,5 kg flat rib, cut into 8 portions

TOMATO GLAZE
125 mℓ (½ cup) tomato sauce
60 mℓ (¼ cup) honey
10 mℓ (2 teaspoons) Worcestershire sauce
15 mℓ (1 tablespoon) soy sauce
15 mℓ (1 tablespoon) white vinegar

Mix together the ingredients for the glaze. Braai the flat rib over moderate coals for about 30 minutes, basting the meat frequently with the glaze.
Serves 8

Corned beef short rib with wine sauce (back) and Glazed flat rib

Veal kidneys on a skottel

4 veal kidneys
6 rashers rindless streaky bacon,
    quartered
1 onion, sliced
150 g button mushrooms
freshly ground black pepper to taste
5 mℓ (1 teaspoon) paprika

Soak the kidneys in cold water for about 30 minutes, then remove the membrane and hard inner core. Pat dry and cut into cubes. Fry the bacon on a skottel braai until it is crisp, then remove it and fry the kidneys for 8 - 10 minutes until nearly cooked. Add the onion and mushrooms and fry for about 5 minutes, until the onion, mushrooms and kidneys are done. Return the bacon to the skottel and season with pepper and paprika.
Serves 4

┌─*HINT*──────────────────────────
To remove some of the strong flavour of the kidneys, soak them for 30 minutes in cold water to which the juice of half a lemon or 5 mℓ (1 teaspoon) vinegar has been added.
└───────────────────────────────

Veal kidneys on a skottel (back) and Liver and bacon

Liver and bacon

500 g ox liver (membrane removed),
    sliced
6 rashers rindless bacon
2 tomatoes, sliced
salt and freshly ground black pepper
    to taste
15 mℓ (1 tablespoon) freshly chopped or
    5 mℓ (1 teaspoon) dried marjoram

Fry the liver on a skottel braai for about 12 minutes, then add the bacon and fry for another 2 minutes. Add the tomato slices and cook for 3 minutes longer. Season with salt, pepper and marjoram, and serve.
Serves 6

┌─*HINT*──────────────────────────
To prepare liver, soak it in milk or salted water for 1 - 2 hours. Rinse quickly under cold water and then carefully remove the outer membrane. If it does not pull away easily, soak it in cold water for a while and try again.
└───────────────────────────────

Veal cushions

Veal cushions

4 large leg of veal steaks, 5 mm thick
5 mℓ (1 teaspoon) salt
freshly ground black pepper to taste
4 slices ham
4 slices cheese (Cheddar or Gruyère)
15 mℓ (1 tablespoon) freshly chopped or
    5 mℓ (1 teaspoon) dried sage
30 mℓ (2 tablespoons) cooking oil

Flatten the meat slightly with a mallet and season with salt and pepper. Place a slice of ham and then a slice of cheese on top of each steak and sprinkle with sage. Fold over and secure with toothpicks. Brush the cushions with oil and braai over moderate coals for about 15 minutes or until done.
Serves 4

Butterfly chops with Parmesan butter (left) and Garlic lamb chops

LAMB

Crispy brown on the outside, slightly pink, tender and succulent inside – nothing can compare with the flavour of lamb hot from the coals. And this versatile meat can be braaied as chops, as a whole leg or shoulder on a spit, as a juicy saddle or a crisp ribbetjie, or as sosaties or kebabs. Whichever form it takes, tasty lamb goes well with a wide variety of foods and is a perennial favourite at any braai.

If you are in a hurry to start braaiing you can do so before the flames of the fire have died down completely – but place the grid high above the flames so that they don't touch the meat.

Garlic lamb chops

8 thick rib chops, 20 mm thick (rib, loin or chump chops can also be used)
2 cloves garlic, crushed

WINE BASTE
125 mℓ (½ cup) dry white wine
5 mℓ (1 teaspoon) freshly chopped or 2 mℓ (a pinch) dried oregano
salt and freshly ground black pepper to taste

Mix together the ingredients for the baste. Slash the fat edges of the chops and rub the garlic onto the meat surface. Braai the chops immediately over moderate coals for 10 - 12 minutes, basting them frequently.
Serves 4

VARIATION
Instead of basting with the wine mixture, these chops can be served with 250 mℓ (1 cup) Tomato sauce (page 86).

Butterfly chops with Parmesan butter

6 butterfly loin chops, 20 mm thick
salt and freshly ground black pepper to taste

PARMESAN BUTTER
60 g (¼ cup) butter
30 mℓ (2 tablespoons) grated Parmesan cheese
5 mℓ (1 teaspoon) lemon juice

To make the Parmesan butter, mix together the butter, cheese and lemon juice. Place the butter on a piece of cling wrap or foil, shape it into a roll, wrap it and freeze for about 1 hour, or until firm. Slash the fat edges of the chops and braai them over moderate coals for 10 - 12 minutes. Season with salt and pepper, and place a pat of butter on each chop. Serve immediately.
Serves 6

Lamb noisettes with brinjals

6 noisettes, 25 mm thick (see page 9)
30 ml (2 tablespoons) butter, melted
6 slices brinjal, 20 mm thick
parsley to garnish

BACON SAUCE
3 rashers rindless bacon, chopped
½ green pepper, chopped
30 ml (2 tablespoons) cake flour
250 ml (1 cup) meat or chicken stock,
    heated

To make the sauce, fry the bacon in a heavy-based pan or potjie, or on a skottel braai. Remove the bacon and fry the green pepper in the bacon fat until it is almost soft. Return the bacon to the pan and stir in the flour. Add the meat stock gradually and let the mixture simmer until it is thick and smooth, stirring all the time. Keep the sauce warm. Braai the noisettes over moderate coals for about 12 minutes. While they are cooking, brush melted butter onto the brinjal slices and braai for about 3 minutes. Place a brinjal slice on top of each noisette and pour some sauce over. Garnish with parsley and serve immediately.
Serves 6

Lamb noisettes with brinjals

Stuffed chump chops

6 chump chops, 20 mm thick
salt and freshly ground black pepper
    to taste

BACON STUFFING
4 rashers rindless bacon, finely chopped
1 small onion, finely chopped
50 g Cheddar cheese, grated (125 ml)
125 ml (½ cup) fresh breadcrumbs
50 ml (3 tablespoons) sour cream

To make the stuffing, fry the bacon and onion gently in a heavy-based pan or potjie, or on a skottel braai until the onion is translucent. Mix in the remaining ingredients and leave to cool. Make an incision in each chop to form a pocket, stuff the chops and secure with toothpicks. Braai the chops over moderate coals for about 15 minutes, then season with salt and pepper.
Serves 6

Lamb chops in yoghurt marinade (back) and Stuffed chump chops

Lamb chops in yoghurt marinade

8 thick rib chops, 20 mm thick (rib, loin
    or chump chops can also be used)

YOGHURT MARINADE
250 ml (1 cup) natural yoghurt
15 ml (1 tablespoon) lemon juice or
    vinegar
50 ml (3 tablespoons) orange juice
15 ml (1 tablespoon) freshly chopped or
    5 ml (1 teaspoon) dried mint
15 ml (1 tablespoon) freshly chopped or
    5 ml (1 teaspoon) dried tarragon
5 ml (1 teaspoon) salt
freshly ground black pepper to taste

Slash the fat edges of the chops. Mix together the marinade ingredients and marinade the chops for about 4 hours. Braai them over moderate coals for 10 - 12 minutes, basting frequently with the marinade.
Serves 4

VARIATION
Curry marinade: Try marinating the chops in 500 ml (2 cups) Basic marinade (page 12), using red wine, and adding 5 ml (1 teaspoon) curry powder and 30 ml (2 tablespoons) smooth apricot jam.

┌─**HINT**─
Serve any Yoghurt marinade that is left over with potatoes cooked in foil on the fire.

Chops in a packet

Chops in a packet

8 thick rib mutton chops, 20 mm thick
  (rib, loin or chump chops can also be
  used)
15 mℓ (1 tablespoon) cooking oil
2 onions, finely chopped
3 tomatoes, peeled and chopped
30 mℓ (2 tablespoons) fruit chutney
5 mℓ (1 teaspoon) salt
freshly ground black pepper to taste

Place each chop on the shiny side of a large
piece of foil. Heat the cooking oil in a heavy-
based saucepan or potjie, or on a skottel
braai and fry the onion gently until it is
translucent. Add the tomato, chutney, salt
and pepper, and let the mixture simmer for
5 minutes. Spoon some tomato mixture on
top of each chop, wrap the foil securely
around it and place the packet over hot
coals, leaving it for 30 minutes.
Serves 4

---HINT---
*To make sure the chops lose none of their
braaied appearance and flavour, brown them
quickly over hot coals before placing them on
the foil.*

Cheese-layered cutlets

8 lamb cutlets, 20 mm thick

CHEESE LAYER
125 mℓ (½ cup) fresh breadcrumbs
1 small onion, finely chopped
15 mℓ (1 tablespoon) freshly chopped or
  5 mℓ (1 teaspoon) dried rosemary
50 g Cheddar cheese, grated (125 mℓ)
60 mℓ (¼ cup) mayonnaise

Mix together the ingredients for the cheese
layer. Braai the cutlets over moderate coals
for 10 - 12 minutes, then spoon a little of the
cheese mixture onto each cutlet and return
them to the grid for another 2 minutes.
Serves 8

---HINT---
*The neat appearance of cutlets (see page 9)
makes them particularly suitable for special
occasions.*

Cheese-layered cutlets

Breast of lamb with braai sauce

1 breast of lamb, about 1 kg

BRAAI SAUCE
30 ml (2 tablespoons) soy sauce
30 ml (2 tablespoons) honey
30 ml (2 tablespoons) dry white wine or vinegar
5 ml (1 teaspoon) Worcestershire sauce
5 ml (1 teaspoon) dry mustard
5 ml (1 teaspoon) tomato paste
5 ml (1 teaspoon) lemon juice

Ask your butcher to saw through the bone at about 20 mm intervals so that the meat can be cut into portions when it is cooked. Mix together the ingredients for the sauce. Braai the meat over moderate coals for about 30 minutes, basting it frequently with the sauce for the last 10 minutes. Cut the meat into portions. Heat the remaining braai sauce and serve it with the meat.
Serves 4

> **HINT**
> *A baste with any sweet ingredient tends to scorch, so brush it on only towards the end of the cooking time.*

Soutribbetjie

1 breast of lamb, 1-1,5 kg
lemon slices to serve

WET CURING
1 litre (4 cups) water
225 g (200 ml/¾ cup) coarse salt
10 ml (2 teaspoons) saltpetre
30 ml (2 tablespoons) sugar
10 ml (2 teaspoons) bicarbonate of soda

Ask your butcher to saw through the breast bone so that the meat can be cut into portions when it is ready. Bring the water to the boil and add the salt, saltpetre, sugar and bicarbonate of soda, stirring well until they have dissolved. Let the liquid cool and strain it through a muslin cloth into a glass, earthenware or plastic container. Add the meat and leave it for 2 days in a cool spot or in the refrigerator.

Remove the meat from the liquid and hang it in a well-ventilated spot until it is dry. Then place the ribbetjie in a saucepan, cover it with cold water and bring to the boil. Reduce the heat and simmer for 1½ hours or until the meat is almost tender. Let

Breast of lamb with braai sauce (left) and Soutribbetjie

it cool and, once again, hang it in a cool place until the surface is dry. Braai the ribbetjie over moderate coals for about 10 minutes, until it is brown and crisp. Cut it into portions and serve with lemon slices.
Serves 6

VARIATION
Dry curing is the more traditional way of salting ribbetjies. Mix together the salt, saltpetre, sugar and bicarbonate of soda and, using 30 - 45 g per 500 g of meat, rub the dry mixture into the meat. Put the ribbetjie in a glass, earthenware or plastic container, laying the thicker pieces at the bottom of the dish, and leave it in the refrigerator for 2 - 3 days. Hang the meat in a cool, well-

ventilated place to dry, then continue the method as for wet curing.

Once it has been boiled, the rib can be covered with muslin cloth and left to hang in a well-ventilated spot for up to 1 week.

> **HINT**
> *If the meat on a well-cured ribbetjie is tender it need not be boiled before going onto the braai. When you take the ribbetjie out of the salt mixture rinse it under running water, then soak it in cold water for 30 minutes to get rid of excess salt. Braai it over low coals for about 45 minutes.*
>
> *Alternatively, smoke the ribbetjie (see page 6) after it has been salted.*

Stuffed saddle of lamb on a spit

1 boned saddle of lamb, about 1,5 kg
15 mℓ (1 tablespoon) gelatine

MUSHROOM STUFFING
15 mℓ (1 tablespoon) cooking oil
15 mℓ (1 tablespoon) butter
150 g mushrooms, chopped
1 onion, chopped
1 clove garlic, chopped
15 mℓ (1 tablespoon) freshly chopped
    herbs (rosemary, oregano, marjoram)
    or 5 mℓ (1 teaspoon) dried mixed herbs
250 mℓ (1 cup) fresh breadcrumbs
30 mℓ (2 tablespoons) sherry
7 mℓ (½ tablespoon) salt
freshly ground black pepper to taste

HERB BASTE
125 mℓ (½ cup) Basic baste (page 12),
    using white wine
10 mℓ (2 teaspoons) freshly chopped
    herbs (rosemary, oregano) or 5 mℓ
    (1 teaspoon) dried mixed herbs

To make the stuffing, heat the cooking oil and butter together in a heavy-based pan or potjie or on a skottel braai and fry the mushrooms, onion and garlic until the onion is translucent. Add the remaining ingredients and mix well. Sprinkle the gelatine inside the saddle and spread the stuffing on top, leaving 25 mm clear around the edges. Fold the two flank sides of the meat to come together at the centre and secure with string at 25 mm intervals. Thread the saddle lengthwise onto the spit and place a drip pan underneath it. Roast the saddle for 1 hour about 150 mm above moderate coals. Mix together the ingredients for the herb baste and brush it over the meat frequently during the last 30 minutes. Let the saddle stand in a warm place for 10 minutes before carving it into thin slices across the grain. Heat the remaining baste and pour it over the slices.
Serves 8 - 10

Stuffed saddle of lamb on a spit

Instead of using salt, season with your own combination of herbs in a shaker. Mix together:

15 mℓ (1 tablespoon) garlic powder
5 mℓ (1 teaspoon) dried basil
5 mℓ (1 teaspoon) dried marjoram
5 mℓ (1 teaspoon) dried thyme
5 mℓ (1 teaspoon) dried parsley
5 mℓ (1 teaspoon) dried sage
5 mℓ (1 teaspoon) black pepper
2 mℓ (a pinch) cayenne pepper

Glazed leg of lamb on a spit

1 leg of lamb, about 2 kg

HONEY GLAZE
50 mℓ (3 tablespoons) honey
50 mℓ (3 tablespoons) soy sauce
125 mℓ (½ cup) meat stock
50 mℓ (3 tablespoons) lemon juice
30 mℓ (2 tablespoons) cooking oil
2 cloves garlic, finely chopped
5 mℓ (1 teaspoon) freshly chopped or 2 mℓ (a pinch) dried oregano

Remove the two bones (the shank and the pelvic bone) at either end of the leg, leaving the marrow bone in the middle. Thread the spit through the centre of the leg, parallel to the marrow bone and tie string around the thicker part of the meat to make the shape of the joint as even as possible. Place a drip pan beneath the meat and arrange the coals around it. Spit-roast the joint for 1½ hours about 150 mm above moderate coals, adding fresh coals from your second fire every half hour or so to maintain a constant temperature. Mix together the glaze ingredients and baste the leg frequently during the last 30 minutes. When the leg is ready, remove it from the spit and leave it in a warm place for 15 minutes. Then carve it into thin slices across the grain of the meat. Combine the remaining glaze with the meat juices in the pan, heat and serve this sauce with the meat.
Serves 8 - 10

HINT
The cooking time can be shortened to 1 - 1¼ hours if the leg of lamb is braaied in a covered grill. To check whether the leg is ready, insert a meat thermometer into the thickest part of the meat (without touching the bone). For medium done meat the thermometer should register 65 °C.

Glazed leg of lamb on a spit

Orange-flavoured shoulder of lamb

Orange-flavoured shoulder of lamb

1 boned shoulder of lamb, about 1 kg (boned leg of lamb can also be used)
1 clove garlic, cut into slivers

ORANGE MARINADE
500 mℓ (2 cups) Basic marinade (page 12), substituting orange juice for half the white wine
15 mℓ (1 tablespoon) freshly chopped or 5 mℓ (1 teaspoon) dried rosemary or marjoram

Cut the boned shoulder open to resemble a butterfly and flatten the meat to an even thickness with a mallet. Make small incisions in the fat and stuff them with garlic slivers. Mix together the ingredients for the orange marinade and marinate the meat for about 5 hours. Braai the shoulder over moderate coals for about 30 minutes, basting frequently with the marinade. Let the meat stand in a warm place for 10 minutes, then carve it into thin slices across the grain.
Serves 6

HINT
The cooking time is shortened and carving is much easier if a shoulder or leg of lamb is boned.

Lamb's liver in caul fat

Lamb's liver in caul fat

500 g lamb's liver, membrane removed
30 mℓ (2 tablespoons) lemon juice
10 mℓ (2 teaspoons) salt (optional)
freshly ground black pepper to taste
1 x 410 g can pineapple chunks, drained
1 piece caul fat, cut into 20 strips

Cut the liver into 20 strips and sprinkle with lemon juice, salt and pepper. Place a pineapple chunk on each strip and wrap both in a piece of caul fat. Secure with toothpicks. Braai the packets over low coals for about 20 minutes.
Makes 20 packets

VARIATIONS
Lamb's liver in bacon: Use bacon rashers instead of strips of caul fat.

Lamb's liver 'sausage': Score the liver with the tines of a fork and mix it with finely chopped onion and thyme. Spoon the mixture into a piping bag and inject it into sausage casings. Tie the casings with string at 75 mm intervals and braai the 'sausages' over moderate coals for about 10 minutes.

Breast of lamb on a skewer

1 kg breast of lamb, cut across the rib
   bones into strips 25 mm wide
500 g lamb sausage, cut into 50 mm
   chunks
salt and freshly ground black pepper
   to taste

HERB BASTE
50 mℓ (3 tablespoons) lemon juice
30 mℓ (2 tablespoons) cooking oil
15 mℓ (1 tablespoon) freshly chopped
   herbs (rosemary, oregano) or 5 mℓ
   (1 teaspoon) dried mixed herbs

Thread the breast of lamb strips concertina-wise onto wooden skewers with 3 chunks of sausage in each fold. Mix together the ingredients for the baste. Braai the meat over moderate coals for about 20 minutes, basting frequently. Season with salt and pepper.
Serves 6

Breast of lamb on a skewer (back) and Lamb kebabs

SOSATIES AND KEBABS

Popularly regarded as a traditional South African dish, sosaties were, in fact, introduced to this country by the Malay community. They consist of cubes of lamb or mutton marinated in a curry mixture and threaded onto wooden or bamboo skewers alternately with cubes of sheep's tail fat, onion chunks or dried apricots.

Kebabs are well known throughout the world although they originally came from Turkey. Traditionally, cubes of lamb alternate with a variety of vegetables, such as tomato, onion and green pepper chunks, on a metal skewer and the whole kebab is left in a basic marinade for several hours. As well as adding colour and flavour to the kebabs, the vegetables make the meat go further.

Sosaties

1 kg boned lamb or mutton, cut into
  20 mm cubes (leg, thick rib or shoulder
  can be used)
250 g speck or sheep's tail fat, cut into
  20 mm cubes

CURRY MARINADE
15 mℓ (1 tablespoon) cooking oil
2 onions, sliced
1 clove garlic, crushed
15 mℓ (1 tablespoon) curry powder
5 mℓ (1 teaspoon) turmeric
30 mℓ (2 tablespoons) brown sugar
1 mℓ (a dash) cayenne pepper
1 mℓ (a dash) chilli powder
125 mℓ (½ cup) dried apricots, or 30 mℓ
  (2 tablespoons) smooth apricot jam
500 mℓ (2 cups) vinegar

To make the marinade, heat the cooking oil in a heavy-based pan and fry the onion and garlic until the onion is translucent. Add the curry powder and turmeric and fry gently. Stir in the sugar, cayenne pepper, chilli powder, apricots and vinegar and simmer for 10 minutes. Let the marinade cool for a few minutes before pouring it over the meat and then leave it in the refrigerator for 1 or 2 days. Stir the meat in the marinade from time to time to make sure all the cubes are well coated. Thread the cubes of meat and speck alternately onto wooden skewers, allowing enough space between them so that they cook evenly. Cover the ends of the skewers with foil to prevent the wood from scorching. Braai the sosaties over low coals for about 20 minutes. Serve immediately.
Serves 6

VARIATION
Substitute 250 mℓ (1 cup) milk for half the vinegar in the marinade to give a slightly milder flavour.

Lamb kebabs

800 g boned leg or shoulder of lamb, cut
  into 20 mm cubes
4 tomatoes, quartered, or 16 cherry
  tomatoes
16 button mushrooms

KEBAB MARINADE
1 x 115 g can tomato paste
125 mℓ (½ cup) cooking oil
250 mℓ (1 cup) dry white wine
100 mℓ (6 tablespoons) honey
10 mℓ (2 teaspoons) freshly chopped or
  3 mℓ (a pinch) dried rosemary
10 mℓ (2 teaspoons) freshly chopped or
  3 mℓ (a pinch) dried oregano
2 cloves garlic, crushed
5 mℓ (1 teaspoon) salt
freshly ground black pepper to taste

Mix together the marinade ingredients. Thread the meat and vegetables alternately onto 8 wooden skewers and leave them in the marinade for 4 hours. Braai the kebabs over low coals for 20 minutes, basting them with the marinade towards the end of the cooking time. Heat the remaining marinade and serve it with the kebabs as soon as they come off the fire.
Serves 8

VARIATION
Green pepper chunks, pineapple chunks, pickling onions, brinjal cubes, prunes or halved kidneys can also be included on a kebab.

Sosaties

Pork chops with thyme butter and Pork chops with cucumber sauce

PORK

Take lean, tender pork and braai it over moderate coals – and you have a dish that is both nutritious and low in kilojoules. Because pork is so lean it tends to dry out, so be gentle in the cooking and generous if you are using a baste. The delicate flavour can well be enhanced by marinating, or complemented by a sauce, especially a fruity one.

To make a favourite braai treat, score the rind of unmarinated pork (if the rind is wet it will become tough rather than crisp), rub salt into it and turn it to the coals for a few minutes at the end of the cooking time. The result – crisp crackling that everyone will enjoy.

Pork chops with thyme butter

6 - 8 pork thick rib chops, 20 mm thick (rib, loin or chump chops can also be used)

THYME BUTTER
60 g (¼ cup) butter
5 mℓ (1 teaspoon) lemon juice
15 mℓ (1 tablespoon) freshly chopped or 5 mℓ (1 teaspoon) dried thyme
2 mℓ (a pinch) grated lemon rind
salt and freshly ground black pepper to taste

To make the thyme butter, beat the butter to soften it and then whip in the remaining ingredients, mixing well. Place the butter on a piece of foil, shape it into a roll, wrap it and place it in the freezer for about 20 minutes. Cut it into slices as you need it. Slash the fat edges of the chops and braai them over moderate coals for 14 - 16 minutes. Serve them immediately with a pat of thyme butter on each.
Serves 6 - 8

HINT
Melt some of the butter and brush it over the chops while they are braaiing.

Pork chops with cucumber sauce

6 pork thick rib chops, 20 mm thick (rib, loin or chump chops can also be used)

CUCUMBER SAUCE
½ English cucumber, seeded, grated and drained
125 mℓ (½ cup) natural yoghurt
15 mℓ (1 tablespoon) freshly chopped or 5 mℓ (1 teaspoon) dried dill or mint
5 mℓ (1 teaspoon) lemon juice
2 mℓ (a pinch) salt
white pepper to taste

Mix together all the ingredients for the sauce and chill it. Slash the fat edges of the chops and braai them over moderate coals for 14 - 16 minutes. Serve the chilled sauce with the chops straight from the grid.
Serves 6

Pork and apple bake

6 pork thick rib chops, 20 mm thick (rib,
   loin or chump chops can also be used)
1 sweet potato, sliced
2 apples, cored and sliced thickly
7 mℓ (½ tablespoon) salt
freshly ground black pepper to taste
70 g (5 tablespoons) butter
75 mℓ (5 tablespoons) brown sugar

Brown the chops quickly on each side, then
put each one on the shiny side of a greased
piece of foil. Lay sweet potato and apple
slices on top and season with salt and pepper. Add a pat of butter and sprinkle brown
sugar over before folding the foil to make a
secure parcel. Place the packets on a grid
over hot coals for about 30 minutes, turning
them frequently during the cooking time.
Serves 6

Pork and apple bake (back) and Stuffed loin chops

> **HINT**
> *If the rib bones of the chops are very sharp
> and likely to pierce the packet, cover the ends
> with a double layer of foil.*

Stuffed loin chops

8 pork loin chops, 30 mm thick (chump
   chops can also be used)
salt and freshly ground black pepper
   to taste

HAM AND MUSHROOM STUFFING
30 mℓ (2 tablespoons) butter
80 g ham, chopped
1 medium onion, chopped
100 g mushrooms, chopped
15 mℓ (1 tablespoon) chopped parsley
15 mℓ (1 tablespoon) lemon juice
3 mℓ (a pinch) salt
freshly ground black pepper to taste
1 mℓ (a dash) cayenne pepper

To make the stuffing, melt the butter in a
heavy-based saucepan or potjie, or on a
skottel braai and fry the ham, onion and
mushrooms until the onion is translucent.
Add the remaining ingredients, mix well
and put the stuffing on one side to cool. Cut
a pocket in each of the chops, stuff them
and secure the openings with toothpicks.
Braai the chops over moderate coals for
14 - 16 minutes, then season with salt and
pepper and serve immediately.
Serves 8

Pork and figs

Pork and figs

8 pork thick rib chops, 20 mm thick (rib,
   loin or chump chops can also be used)

FIG BASTE
1 x 410 g can figs or 6 fresh figs
30 mℓ (2 tablespoons) soy sauce
30 mℓ (2 tablespoons) dry white wine
15 mℓ (1 tablespoon) Worcestershire sauce
3 mℓ (a pinch) dry mustard
½ medium onion, grated

To make the baste, pour the figs with half of
the syrup from the can into a blender. Add
the soy sauce, wine, Worcestershire sauce
and mustard, and liquidise. Pour the liquid
into a saucepan and add the grated onion.
Bring the mixture to the boil, then lower the
heat and simmer without a lid for 5 minutes. Slash the fat edges of the chops and
braai them over moderate coals for 14 - 16
minutes, brushing them frequently with
the fig baste. Heat the remaining baste and
serve it with the chops.
Serves 8

> **HINT**
> *Apricots, peaches, pawpaw, pineapple, kiwi
> fruit, oranges, prunes and apples are all
> fruits that go exceptionally well with pork.*

Savoury spareribs (back) and Breast of pork in pineapple marinade

Kasseler rib in foil

Savoury spareribs

1 kg pork spareribs, sawn into portions
salt and freshly ground black pepper
    to taste

SAVOURY MARINADE
125 mℓ (½ cup) cooking oil
250 mℓ (1 cup) rooibos tea
125 mℓ (½ cup) tomato sauce
125 mℓ (½ cup) chutney
30 mℓ (2 tablespoons) Worcestershire
    sauce
60 mℓ (¼ cup) wine vinegar
1 clove garlic, chopped
5 mℓ (1 teaspoon) prepared mustard
1 onion, chopped

Mix the marinade ingredients in a saucepan, bring to the boil and let simmer for a few minutes. Let the liquid cool and marinate the spareribs in it for 4 hours. When you have taken the meat out of the marinade pat it dry with paper towel. Braai the spareribs over moderate coals for 20 - 25 minutes, basting them frequently with the remaining marinade. Season with salt and pepper.
Serves 6

Breast of pork in pineapple marinade

1 kg breast of pork (rind removed), sawn
    into portions

PINEAPPLE MARINADE
250 mℓ (1 cup) dry white wine
30 mℓ (2 tablespoons) cooking oil
1 x 410 g can crushed pineapple or 375 mℓ
    (1½ cups) grated fresh pineapple
15 mℓ (1 tablespoon) soy sauce
5 mℓ (1 teaspoon) lemon juice
3 mℓ (a pinch) dry mustard
50 mℓ (3 tablespoons) honey
15 mℓ (1 tablespoon) Worcestershire sauce
1 clove garlic, crushed

Mix the marinade ingredients in a saucepan, bring to the boil and let simmer for 2 - 3 minutes. Let the liquid cool and then marinate the portions of breast in it for 4 hours. When you have taken the meat out of the marinade pat it dry with paper towel. Braai the meat over moderate coals for 20 - 25 minutes, basting it frequently with the marinade.
Serves 6

Kasseler rib in foil

6 kasseler rib chops, 20 mm thick
15 mℓ (1 tablespoon) prepared mustard
30 mℓ (2 tablespoons) brown sugar
6 whole cloves
1 x 440 g can pineapple rings
60 g (¼ cup) butter

Place each chop on the shiny side of a greased piece of foil. Spread mustard on the chops and sprinkle brown sugar over. Stick a clove into each pineapple ring, put a ring on each chop and top with a dollop of butter. Wrap the foil securely around each chop and leave the packets on a grid over hot coals for 20 minutes.
Serves 6

Butterfly saddle of pork

1 saddle of pork, about 2 kg
salt and freshly ground black pepper
    to taste

GINGER MARINADE
5 mℓ (1 teaspoon) grated lemon rind
15 mℓ (1 tablespoon) chopped root ginger
50 mℓ (3 tablespoons) olive oil or
    cooking oil
15 mℓ (1 tablespoon) soy sauce
2 - 3 cloves garlic, crushed
15 mℓ (1 tablespoon) chopped fresh mint
2 mℓ (a pinch) salt

Cut any excess fat off the pork, bone the
meat and place it on a wooden board with
the fat side down. Cover the meat with a
sheet of greaseproof paper and flatten it
with a mallet. Pound the marinade ingredients to a paste with a pestle and mortar,
spread the marinade on the meat and leave
it to stand for 1 hour. Braai the saddle over
hot coals for about 40 minutes, turning it
frequently. Season with salt and pepper,
and carve the meat into thin slices. Serve
chilled Pawpaw purée (page 88) with the
saddle.
Serves 8

Saratoga chops with plum glaze

1,2 kg boned pork loin
10 mℓ (2 teaspoons) salt
freshly ground black pepper to taste

PLUM GLAZE
1 x 410 g can plums, drained and chopped
5 mℓ (1 teaspoon) ground ginger
15 mℓ (1 tablespoon) brown sugar
15 mℓ (1 tablespoon) brandy

Sprinkle half the salt and pepper on the inside of the loin, roll it up and insert skewers
at 25 mm intervals through the roll. Cut the
roll into slices halfway between each pair of
skewers. Mix together the ingredients for
the glaze. Braai the saratoga chops over
moderate coals for 16 - 18 minutes, basting
them frequently with the glaze. Season
with the remaining salt and pepper.
Serves 6

*Butterfly saddle of pork (left) and Saratoga chops
with plum glaze*

Pork kebabs in pawpaw marinade

1,5 kg boned thick rib of pork, cut into 25 mm cubes
salt and freshly ground black pepper to taste

PAWPAW MARINADE
1 small pawpaw, peeled and cut into chunks
250 mℓ (1 cup) orange juice
5 mℓ (1 teaspoon) grated orange rind
75 mℓ (5 tablespoons) cooking oil
2 mℓ (a pinch) salt
10 mℓ (2 teaspoons) mild curry powder

To make the marinade, place the ingredients in a blender and liquidise them. Thread the cubes of meat onto 6 skewers and marinate them for 4 hours. When you take the kebabs out of the marinade pat them dry with paper towel. Braai them over moderate coals for about 20 minutes, basting frequently with the marinade. Season with salt and pepper before serving.
Serves 6

┌─**HINT**──────────────────────────┐
│ *Do not marinate the kebabs overnight be-* │
│ *cause a marinade containing pawpaw tends* │
│ *to set.* │
└──────────────────────────────────┘

Concertina kebabs

1 kg belly of pork, cut into strips 25 mm wide
12 - 15 pickling onions
salt and freshly ground black pepper to taste

BEER MARINADE
250 mℓ (1 cup) sour cream
250 mℓ (1 cup) beer
30 mℓ (2 tablespoons) chopped root ginger or 10 mℓ (2 teaspoons) ground ginger
5 mℓ (1 teaspoon) salt
freshly ground black pepper to taste
30 mℓ (2 tablespoons) lemon juice
2 cloves garlic, crushed

Thread the meat strips concertina-wise onto wooden skewers with a pickling onion in each fold. Mix together the marinade ingredients and marinate the kebabs overnight in the refrigerator. Pat the meat dry with paper towel when you take it out of the marinade. Braai the kebabs over moderate coals for about 20 minutes, basting them frequently with the marinade. Season with salt and pepper and serve immediately.
Serves 6

Left to right: Pork kebabs in pawpaw marinade, Pork kebabs, Mixed grill on a skewer and Concertina kebabs

Pork kebabs

500 - 700 g boned leg of pork, cut into
    20 mm cubes
4 rashers rindless bacon, halved and
    rolled up
1 pimiento, seeded and cubed
16 cherry tomatoes or 2 large tomatoes,
    seeded and quartered
16 pickling onions
salt and freshly ground black pepper
    to taste

SPICY MARINADE
60 mℓ (¼ cup) soy sauce
30 mℓ (2 tablespoons) honey
60 mℓ (¼ cup) medium cream sherry
5 mℓ (1 teaspoon) ground cinnamon
freshly ground black pepper to taste
2 mℓ (a pinch) ground cloves
1 clove garlic, crushed
60 mℓ (¼ cup) rooibos tea, chilled

Mix together the ingredients for the marinade and marinate the pork for 4 - 5 hours. Pat the meat dry with paper towel when you take it out of the marinade and thread the cubes alternately with the bacon rolls and vegetables onto skewers. Braai the kebabs over moderate coals for about 15 minutes, basting them frequently with the marinade. Season with salt and pepper and serve immediately.
Makes 8 kebabs

Mixed grill on a skewer

500 g boned leg of pork or thick rib
500 g beef fillet or Scotch fillet
500 g Mutton sausage (page 37)
6 - 8 sheep's kidneys (membrane and core
    removed), halved
125 mℓ (½ cup) Basic baste (page 12),
    using white wine
salt and freshly ground black pepper

Wrap the leg of pork and the fillet loosely in cling wrap or foil and place in the freezer for about 20 minutes. Cut the meat into thin slices and roll up each slice. Thread the Mutton sausage concertina-wise onto skewers, placing the pork, fillet and kidneys alternately in each fold. Braai the kebabs over moderate coals for 20 minutes, brushing them frequently with Basic baste. Season to taste with salt and pepper and serve immediately.
Serves 6

┌─**HINT**────────────────────────┐
To give extra flavour, use a sprig of rosemary or fresh bay leaves instead of a brush for basting.
└─────────────────────────────┘

Clockwise from top right: Liver sausage, Mutton sausage, Frankfurters, Pork sausage and Boerewors

SAUSAGES

For many South Africans 'boerewors', a traditional sausage made of minced beef and pork suitably spiced, is a must for every braai. The preferred flavour of boerewors is a very personal matter and if you want to be sure that the boerewors you braai is completely to your liking, the best way is to make your own.

With the correct equipment – a mincer and a sausage filler – this is not difficult to do, and the satisfaction of serving delicious homemade boerewors at your braai is definitely worth the effort!

Freshly smoked foods are delicious, but try keeping the smoked food for at least 24 hours – the flavour then is even better.

THE MINCER

Make sure the mincer blade and plate are sharp before you begin. A plate with 9 mm holes gives minced meat with the correct texture for boerewors.

THE MEAT

Cut the meat into 50 mm cubes, spread the cubes on a large, clean surface, sprinkle the spices over and mix lightly before mincing. Too much stirring and kneading gives a sausage that has a rubbery texture and is more like polony than 'wors'.

THE SPICES

The special ingredient in any sausage is fresh spice. Coriander is traditionally used in boerewors and ideally should be freshly scorched and ground. A pestle and mortar, a pepper mill and a nutmeg grater are all essential items of equipment for the successful sausage-maker.

THE CASING

Sausage casing can be bought from most butchers. If you buy it frozen, soak it in lukewarm water for about an hour, then rinse it under cold running water and drain well. When filling, take care to eliminate air bubbles, but don't fill too tightly or the casing will burst during cooking. Use mutton, rather than pork, casing if you prefer thinner sausages.

THE FLAVOUR

The flavour, and texture, improve immeasurably if the sausage is refrigerated for at least one day before braaiing so that the flavour of the spices can permeate the meat thoroughly. Boerewors should not be frozen for longer than two months as changes in the flavour may occur.

BRAAIING SAUSAGES

'Wors' is best braaied slowly over moderate coals, and best removed from the heat just before it is cooked right through, as the cooking process will continue on its own for a short time. To prevent juice from escaping, keep the lengths of sausage as long as is manageable – you will find them easier to handle as coils on the grid – and avoid piercing the casing.

Boerewors

2 kg boneless chuck of beef
750 g boneless thick rib of pork
200 g speck
15 mℓ (1 tablespoon) ground coriander
30 mℓ (2 tablespoons) fine salt
5 mℓ (1 teaspoon) freshly ground black
 pepper
2 mℓ (a pinch) freshly grated nutmeg
100 mℓ (6 tablespoons) vinegar
90 g pork casings

Cut the meat and speck into 50 mm cubes. Combine the coriander, seasoning and nutmeg, sprinkle over the cubes and mix well. Mince the meat and speck, then add the vinegar and mix lightly but thoroughly. Stuff into the casing and refrigerate. Braai over low coals for about 15 minutes.
Makes 3 kg

VARIATION
To make sausage with a coarser texture, dice the speck and add it to the meat after it has been minced.

┌─*HINT*──────────────────────────┐
│ To scorch coriander, place the seeds in a dry
│ frying pan and heat, stirring constantly,
│ until they become light brown. Grind them
│ in a blender or with a pestle and mortar, or
│ with a rolling pin crush them between two
│ pieces of cloth. Pass them through a sieve to
│ remove the husks. Crush 15 mℓ (1 table-
│ spoon) whole coriander to obtain 5 mℓ (1 tea-
│ spoon) ground coriander.
└────────────────────────────────┘

Mutton sausage

5 kg leg or thick rib of mutton
500 g sheep's tail fat (if the mutton
 is lean)
30 - 50 mℓ (2 - 3 tablespoons) fine salt
10 mℓ (2 teaspoons) freshly ground white
 pepper
30 mℓ (2 tablespoons) freshly ground
 coriander
20 - 25 mℓ (1½ - 2 tablespoons) allspice
125 mℓ (½ cup) white vinegar
90 g pork or mutton casing

Cut the meat and fat into 50 mm cubes. Mix together the seasoning and spices and sprinkle them over the meat. Mince, add the vinegar and mix lightly but thoroughly. Stuff loosely into the casing and refrigerate. Braai over low coals for about 10 minutes.
Makes 5 kg

VARIATION
Curried mutton sausage: Add 50 mℓ (3 tablespoons) mild curry powder to the sausage mixture.

Pork sausage

3 kg boneless thick rib of pork
30 mℓ (2 tablespoons) fine salt
5 mℓ (1 teaspoon) freshly ground white
 pepper
2 mℓ (a pinch) ground cloves
5 mℓ (1 teaspoon) freshly ground
 coriander
2 mℓ (a pinch) freshly grated nutmeg
125 mℓ (½ cup) vinegar
90 g pork casing

Cut the meat into 50 mm cubes, sprinkle the seasoning and spices over and mix well. Mince the meat, add the vinegar and mix lightly but thoroughly. Stuff into the casing and refrigerate. Braai over low coals for about 15 minutes.
Makes 3 kg

┌─*HINT*──────────────────────────┐
│ Mince the meat twice if you like a finer
│ texture.
└────────────────────────────────┘

Liver sausage

1 kg ox liver, minced
50 g speck, finely diced
1 onion, chopped
7 mℓ (½ tablespoon) salt
freshly ground black pepper to taste
15 mℓ (1 tablespoon) freshly chopped or
 5 mℓ (1 teaspoon) dried thyme
10 mℓ (2 teaspoons) lemon juice
50 g casing

Mix together all the ingredients, stuff the mixture into the casing and twist the sausage into 100 mm lengths. Knot the casing at both ends. Braai over low coals for about 12 minutes. Serve immediately.
Makes 1 kg

Smoked sausages

8 pork sausages or 500 g boerewors
a large handful of wood chips (e.g.
 hickory, oak, peach, pear or apple
 woods)

Place the wood chips in the bottom of a heavy-based saucepan, put a round cooling tray on top and arrange the sausage on the tray, allowing space between the individual sausages or the coils of sausage. Cover the saucepan with a tight-fitting lid and place on a grid over hot coals. Smoke the sausage for 15 minutes, keeping the lid in place. Remove the saucepan from the heat and allow to stand for 5 minutes before removing the lid.
Serves 4

┌─*HINT*──────────────────────────┐
│ This is a quick method of smoking if a smok-
│ ing dome is not available.
└────────────────────────────────┘

Frankfurters

1,5 kg boneless thick rib or leg of pork
freshly ground black pepper to taste
15 mℓ (1 tablespoon) fine salt
1 mℓ (a dash) freshly grated nutmeg
1 mℓ (a dash) freshly ground coriander
50 mℓ (3 tablespoons) dry red wine
60 g mutton or pork casing

Cut the meat into cubes, sprinkle the seasoning and spices over and mince the cubes twice. Add the wine and mix lightly but thoroughly. Stuff into the casing and smoke for about 4 hours or until the sausages are a rich golden brown (see page 6).
Makes 1,5 kg

Savoury sausage dish

500 g cooked sausage
15 mℓ (1 tablespoon) cooking oil
1 large onion, sliced into rings
1 clove garlic, chopped
1 small green pepper, cut into strips
1 brinjal, diced
200 mℓ (¾ cup) meat stock
1 x 410 g can baked beans in tomato sauce
salt and freshly ground black pepper
 to taste

Cut the sausage into 20 mm chunks. Heat the cooking oil in a heavy-based saucepan or potjie, or on a skottel braai and fry the onion, garlic, green pepper and brinjal until the onion is translucent. Add the meat stock and simmer for a few minutes. Mix in the sausage chunks and beans, season with salt and pepper and heat thoroughly. Serve with fresh bread, noodles or rice.
Serves 6

Basic hamburgers

500 g lean minced beef
1 onion, chopped
1 apple, peeled and grated
3 mℓ (a pinch) salt
freshly ground black pepper to taste
3 mℓ (a pinch) freshly chopped or 1 mℓ
    (a dash) dried thyme

Mix together all the ingredients lightly with a fork and shape into patties. Braai over moderate coals for about 12 minutes or until done.
Serves 8

VARIATIONS
Cheese burgers: Grate 60 g Cheddar cheese and add it to the basic mixture.

Herb burgers: Add 15 mℓ (1 tablespoon) chopped parsley, 15 mℓ (1 tablespoon) prepared mustard and 15 mℓ (1 tablespoon) lemon juice to the basic mixture.

To enhance the flavour of the basic hamburger add:
• a dash of Tabasco, Worcestershire sauce, soy sauce, prepared mustard, chutney or tomato paste
• a pinch of paprika, chilli powder, ground coriander, nutmeg, curry powder or cumin
• a dash of brandy, sherry, port, vermouth or red or white wine
• finely chopped green or red pepper, mushrooms, celery, olives, capers or gherkins
    To stretch the burger portion, add 125 mℓ (½ cup) fresh breadcrumbs or mashed potato.

Lamb patties (back) and Basic hamburgers

HAMBURGERS

Hamburgers have the advantages of being quick to braai (a bonus when there are hungry children around), economical to make, and they are extremely versatile. With the variation of an ingredient here and a garnish there, you can present a host of different burgers at once.

When making the patties choose quality lean meat for mincing, adding one third mutton or pork to two thirds beef for extra flavour and succulence. Mince the meat coarsely and don't mould the patties too tightly or they will be rubbery.

Lamb patties

500 g minced lean lamb
3 mℓ (a pinch) salt
freshly ground black pepper to taste
15 mℓ (1 tablespoon) freshly chopped or
    5 mℓ (1 teaspoon) dried mint
1 slice white bread soaked in 75 mℓ
    (5 tablespoons) milk

Mix all the ingredients lightly with a fork and shape into patties. Braai over moderate coals for about 12 minutes or until done.
Serves 8

Tasty tomato mince kebabs (back) and Curry fricadels

Curry fricadels

15 mℓ (1 tablespoon) cooking oil
1 onion, chopped
15 mℓ (1 tablespoon) curry powder
250 g minced pork
250 g minced beef
5 mℓ (1 teaspoon) salt
freshly ground black pepper to taste
30 mℓ (2 tablespoons) chutney

Heat the cooking oil on a skottel braai or in a potjie or heavy-based saucepan over the fire. Fry the onion gently until it is translucent. Add the curry powder and fry for 1 minute longer. Allow to cool, then add the remaining ingredients and mix lightly with a fork. Shape the mixture into patties and braai over moderate coals for about 12 minutes or until done.
Serves 8

Tasty tomato mince kebabs

500 g minced topside of beef
freshly ground black pepper to taste
3 mℓ (a pinch) salt
3 mℓ (a pinch) ground coriander

Mix all the ingredients, kneading them together lightly. Shape the mixture into small sausages around a skewer and braai over moderate coals for about 12 minutes. Serve hot with Tomato sauce (page 86).
Serves 6

┌─HINT──────────────────
│ *If the meat is minced twice it will stick more firmly to the skewer.*
└──────────────────────

Lemon chicken halves (back) and Fruity chicken

CHICKEN

As versatile on the braai as it is in the kitchen, chicken can be cooked as portions either in foil or directly over the coals; it can be stuffed and roasted whole on a spit; or it can be cut into chunks for kebabs. And its delicate flavour blends well with a great variety of marinades, bastes and sauces. Chicken enjoys long, slow cooking so let it take its time. As the fat layer between the skin and flesh melts it helps to keep the meat moist but even so, the bird needs frequent basting. When the flesh is cooked, lower the grid to the coals to brown the skin — and you will end up with a delicious blend of tender meat surrounded by crisp, tasty skin.

Fruity chicken

2 medium chickens
6 ripe peaches, split and stoned
6 ripe apricots, split and stoned

BRANDY-LEMON MARINADE
110 g (½ cup) butter, melted or 125 mℓ
    (½ cup) cooking oil
50 mℓ (3 tablespoons) lemon juice
50 mℓ (3 tablespoons) brandy
30 mℓ (2 tablespoons) brown sugar

Mix together the ingredients for the marinade and soak the peaches and apricots in it for about 1 hour. Drain the fruit and place it in a drip pan. Split the chickens by cutting along the breast bones and place them on a grid over the fire with the drip pan directly beneath the meat. Braai the chickens over moderate coals for about 40 minutes, basting them frequently with the marinade. Stir together the meat juices and fruit in the drip pan and serve this hot with the chicken.
Serves 6

Lemon chicken halves

2 small chickens

LEMON BASTE
110 g (½ cup) butter, melted or
    125 mℓ (5 tablespoons) cooking oil
30 mℓ (2 tablespoons) lemon juice
10 mℓ (2 teaspoons) grated lemon rind
1 clove garlic, crushed
freshly ground white pepper to taste

Split the chickens by cutting them along the breast bones. Mix together the ingredients for the lemon baste and brush some over the chicken. Braai the chicken halves over moderate coals for about 40 minutes, turning and basting them frequently.
Serves 4

VARIATION
Herbs such as marjoram, thyme and parsley may be added to the lemon baste.

┌─**HINT**─────────────
To add flavour to the chicken, throw a piece of lemon or orange rind onto the coals for the last 30 minutes of the cooking time.

Tandoori chicken

8 chicken portions, skinned

YOGHURT MARINADE
250 mℓ (1 cup) natural yoghurt
5 mℓ (1 teaspoon) grated root ginger or
   3 mℓ (a pinch) ground ginger (optional)
5 mℓ (1 teaspoon) paprika
5 mℓ (1 teaspoon) chilli powder
1 clove garlic, crushed
2 peppercorns, slightly crushed
15 mℓ (1 tablespoon) tomato purée
5 mℓ (1 teaspoon) salt
15 mℓ (1 tablespoon) grated lemon rind
15 mℓ (1 tablespoon) lemon juice
2 bay leaves

Mix together the marinade ingredients.
Prick the chicken portions all over with a
fork and marinate them for 24 hours, turning occasionally. Braai the portions over
moderate coals for about 20 minutes, turning them from time to time and basting
them frequently with the marinade.
Serves 4

Spicy chicken wings

8 - 10 chicken wings

SPICY MARINADE
5 rashers rindless bacon, finely chopped
1 onion, finely chopped
125 mℓ (½ cup) tomato juice
15 mℓ (1 tablespoon) Worcestershire or
   soy sauce
3 mℓ (½ teaspoon) prepared mustard
15 mℓ (1 tablespoon) lemon juice
15 mℓ (1 tablespoon) sugar
salt and freshly ground black pepper

To make the marinade, fry the bacon until it
is crisp, then add the onion and fry gently
until the onion is translucent. Add the remaining marinade ingredients and simmer
for 10 minutes. Cool the marinade, pour it
over the chicken wings and leave them for 1
hour. Drain the wings, then braai them over
moderate coals for about 15 minutes, basting them frequently with the marinade.
Serves 4

VARIATION
Thighs or drumsticks can also be cooked
in this way, but braai them for longer,
18 - 20 minutes.

Tandoori chicken (back) and Spicy chicken wings

Above: Honey-glazed chicken thighs

Below: Chicken and vegetable packets

Honey-glazed chicken thighs

**4 large chicken thighs, skinned and
  boned
salt and freshly ground white pepper
  to taste**

**HONEY GLAZE
30 mℓ (2 tablespoons) muscadel or
  hanepoot wine
15 mℓ (1 tablespoon) honey
15 mℓ (1 tablespoon) lemon juice
5 mℓ (1 teaspoon) prepared French
  mustard
5 mℓ (1 teaspoon) freshly chopped herbs
  (thyme, marjoram) or 3 mℓ (a pinch)
  dried mixed herbs**

Season each chicken thigh with salt and
pepper and place it on a buttered piece of
foil, shiny side up. Mix together the ingredients for the glaze and spread it over the
chicken. Seal the parcels well and cook
them among low coals for about 30 minutes. Serve the chicken with its tangy sauce
straight from the foil.
Serves 4

┌─**HINT**─────────────────────
*You don't need to turn the parcels as the heat
is trapped within the foil, cooking the con-
tents from all sides.*
└───────────────────────────

Chicken and vegetable packets

**1 chicken, cut into portions
1 onion, sliced into rings
2 - 3 potatoes, peeled and sliced
2 tomatoes, sliced
150 g mushrooms, sliced
1 green pepper, cut into chunks
10 mℓ (2 teaspoons) salt
freshly ground black pepper to taste
50 mℓ (3 tablespoons) butter**

Place each chicken portion on a buttered
piece of foil, shiny side up. Top the portions
with layers of vegetables and sprinkle salt
and pepper over. Add a dollop of butter to
each parcel, wrap securely and braai on a
grid over moderate coals for about 40 minutes, until the meat is tender and the vegetables are cooked. Serve Mustard sauce
(page 87) with the chicken.
Serves 6

Chicken Kiev over the coals

8 chicken breasts, boned and skinned
50 mℓ (3 tablespoons) butter, melted
salt and freshly ground black pepper

HERB BUTTER
120 g (½ cup) butter
30 mℓ (2 tablespoons) freshly chopped or
   10 mℓ (2 teaspoons) dried tarragon
30 mℓ (2 tablespoons) freshly chopped or
   10 mℓ (2 teaspoons) dried parsley
30 mℓ (2 tablespoons) freshly chopped or
   10 mℓ (2 teaspoons) dried rosemary
15 mℓ (1 tablespoon) lemon juice
salt and freshly ground black pepper
   to taste

Cut the chicken breasts in half lengthwise, place each half between two pieces of greaseproof paper and beat it flat with a mallet. Mix together the ingredients for the herb butter and spread it onto the flattened halves. Roll up each half lengthwise and secure it with toothpicks. Braai the chicken rolls over low coals for 15 - 18 minutes, turning them frequently. Brush them with melted butter and season to taste with salt and pepper before serving.
Serves 4

Mandarin chicken

6 chicken portions

MANDARIN MARINADE
30 mℓ (2 tablespoons) cooking oil
1 onion, finely chopped
2 cloves garlic, crushed
10 mℓ (2 teaspoons) chopped root ginger
   or 3 mℓ (a pinch) ground ginger
1 x 310 g can mandarin oranges, drained
   and chopped
30 mℓ (2 tablespoons) brown sugar
50 mℓ (3 tablespoons) soy sauce
50 mℓ (3 tablespoons) tomato sauce
5 mℓ (1 teaspoon) chicken stock powder

Heat the cooking oil and fry the onion, garlic and ginger gently until the onion is translucent. Add the remaining ingredients and simmer for 5 minutes. Let the liquid cool and marinate the chicken for about 3 hours. Braai the portions over moderate coals for about 20 minutes, basting frequently with the marinade. Heat the remaining marinade and serve it with the chicken.
Serves 6

Chicken Kiev over the coals

Peri-peri chicken (back) and Mandarin chicken

Peri-peri chicken

8 chicken drumsticks (breasts or thighs
   can also be used)
salt to taste

PERI-PERI BASTE
125 mℓ (½ cup) olive oil or cooking oil
2 cloves garlic, crushed
5 mℓ (1 teaspoon) peri-peri
30 mℓ (2 tablespoons) lemon juice

Heat the oil in a heavy-based pan or on a skottel braai, add the garlic and fry gently until golden brown. Stir in the peri-peri and lemon juice, then allow the baste to cool. Braai the drumsticks over moderate coals for about 20 minutes, basting them frequently. Season with salt and serve immediately.
Serves 4

Savoury chicken liver kebabs

125 g rindless streaky bacon
500 g chicken livers
12 cherry tomatoes
125 g button mushrooms
12 prunes, stoned
70 g (5 tablespoons) butter, melted

Wrap a bacon rasher around each chicken liver and secure with a toothpick. Thread the bacon-wrapped livers, tomatoes, mushrooms and prunes alternately onto skewers. Brush with melted butter and braai over moderate coals for about 10 minutes. Serve immediately.
Serves 4

Chicken kebabs

2 chicken breasts, skinned, boned and
   cut into 25 mm cubes
8 pickling onions or 2 medium onions
3 bananas, peeled and quartered
6 rashers rindless streaky bacon, halved
1 pimiento, seeded and cut into cubes

SWEET-SOUR MARINADE
30 mℓ (2 tablespoons) brown sugar
15 mℓ (1 tablespoon) Worcestershire sauce
30 mℓ (2 tablespoons) lemon juice
3 mℓ (a pinch) salt

Mix together the marinade ingredients and marinate the chicken cubes for about 4 hours. Place the onions in boiling water and simmer for 5 minutes. If you are using medium onions, drain and quarter them after boiling. Drain the chicken cubes and reserve the marinade. Wrap each piece of banana in half a bacon rasher and dip it into the marinade. Thread the chicken, bacon-wrapped banana, onions and pimiento alternately onto 4 skewers and brush with the marinade. Braai the kebabs over low coals for 15 - 20 minutes, turning and basting them frequently.
Serves 4

Savoury chicken liver kebabs (left) and Chicken kebabs

Bastes containing sugar are quick to burn and require slow and careful braaiing. Apply them only towards the end of the cooking time.

Chicken on the spit

Ideally the mass of a chicken to be spit-roasted should be between 1 and 1,5 kg, although you can, of course, roast as many chickens at the same time as the length of your spit allows. To spit-roast a whole chicken, tie or skewer the wing tips over the breast and fasten the neck skin to the back with a skewer. Push the spit through the bird from the tail end towards the front so that the point emerges between the branches of the wishbone. Anchor the chicken to the spit by crossing the drumsticks and tying them to the tail. Half chickens should be pierced through the thigh, then the breast meat and firmly anchored. Make sure that the prongs of the spit are firmly in place and that the bird is evenly balanced.

Use a marinade of your choice or any of the following stuffings, or both – but if you use both, remember that their flavours should complement each other. If you choose a stuffing, spoon it into the bird and close the cavity with skewers.

A medium-sized chicken takes about 1 hour to roast. Baste it frequently during the last 20 - 30 minutes. When the bird is ready, the breast meat near the wing joint will be tender and the meat on the drumstick will be soft.

Chicken on the spit

Stuffings for chicken

Ham and veal stuffing

50 mℓ (3 tablespoons) butter
100 g minced veal (beef can be used instead)
100 g cooked ham, finely chopped
1 onion, finely chopped
250 mℓ (1 cup) fresh breadcrumbs
125 mℓ (½ cup) seedless raisins
salt and freshly ground black pepper to taste
1 egg, beaten
50 mℓ (3 tablespoons) dry white wine

Melt the butter in a pan or potjie and fry the veal and ham gently for a few minutes. Add the onion and fry gently until it is translucent. Remove the pan from the heat and allow it to cool slightly. Add the remaining ingredients and mix well.

Apricot stuffing

30 mℓ (2 tablespoons) butter
2 large onions, finely chopped
1 x 410 g can apricots, drained and chopped
500 mℓ (2 cups) cooked rice
1 egg, beaten
3 mℓ (a pinch) dried sage
10 mℓ (2 teaspoons) finely chopped parsley

Melt the butter in a pan or potjie and fry the onion gently until it is translucent. Remove the pan from the heat and allow it to cool. Add the remaining ingredients and mix well.

VARIATION
Pineapple stuffing: Substitute pineapple chunks for the apricots.

Prune stuffing

15 mℓ (1 tablespoon) cooking oil
250 g minced beef
1 onion, chopped
1 egg, beaten
12 prunes, stoned and chopped
50 mℓ (3 tablespoons) chopped walnuts
10 mℓ (2 teaspoons) grated lemon rind
30 mℓ (2 tablespoons) freshly chopped or 10 mℓ (2 teaspoons) dried parsley
salt and freshly ground black pepper

Heat the cooking oil in a saucepan or potjie and fry the mince until it changes colour. Add the onion and fry gently until it is translucent. Remove the pan from the heat and allow it to cool slightly. Add the remaining ingredients and mix well.
Each recipe makes enough for 1 chicken

Galjoen braai

Begin braaiing fillets and 'vlekked' fish with the skin towards the fire so that it protects the flesh and so that the layer of fat between skin and flesh has a chance to melt. When the fish is turned for the last few minutes of the cooking time, this melted fat bastes the flesh, helping to keep it moist.

Galjoen braai

1 fresh galjoen, about 1,5 kg, scaled but not skinned
50 mℓ (3 tablespoons) butter, melted
50 mℓ (3 tablespoons) cooking oil
50 mℓ (3 tablespoons) coarse salt
30 mℓ (2 tablespoons) lemon juice

Vlek open the galjoen (see page 11), leaving intact the stomach area which contains most of the fat. Remove the entrails carefully and wipe the fish clean inside and out. Mix together the butter and cooking oil and a little of the salt, and brush over the skin. Sprinkle the coarse salt generously over the flesh and place the open fish in a well-oiled hinged grid. Braai the galjoen skin down about 300 mm above moderate coals. When the skin is crisp and golden brown turn the fish over and lower the grid to brown the flesh quickly without letting it become dry. Baste with lemon juice from time to time.
Serves 4

---HINT---
Traditionally, galjoen is served with brown bread and grape jam.

FISH

There can be few things in life that give greater pleasure than eating freshly caught and braaied fish within sight and sound of the sea. Even without the sea, a fish braai is an occasion to be savoured.

The best way to braai most fish is whole, with fins and tail intact, on a grid over open coals. Some types, however, benefit from being cooked in foil for, although they lack the smoky braaied flavour and crisp appearance of open-braaied fish, they remain succulent. If you are braaiing fish whole use a fish basket or hinged grid to make handling easier and to prevent the fish from breaking up. Fish is braaied over a cooler fire than meat (or further from the coals) to prevent the skin from scorching.

Seafood selection

Snoek braai

1 fresh snoek, about 2 kg
100 mℓ (6 tablespoons) coarse salt
freshly ground white pepper to taste

LEMON BASTE
juice of 2 large lemons
60 g (¼ cup) butter, melted

Vlek the snoek (see page 11), sprinkle the flesh liberally with coarse salt and leave it for 30 minutes to 1 hour, depending on how heavily salted you like the fish. Rinse off the salt with fresh water and hang the fish to dry. Mix together the lemon juice and butter. Season the snoek lightly with pepper and place it open in a well-oiled hinged grid. Braai skin down over low coals, brushing a lean fish with the lemon baste. When the flesh becomes white turn the fish over to brown it slightly. Serve immediately.
Serves 8

HINT

A popular accompaniment to braaied snoek is whole sweet potatoes baked in foil amongst the coals (see page 79).

Braaied snoek with apricot baste

1 fresh snoek, about 2 kg
salt and freshly ground black pepper
   to taste

APRICOT BASTE
50 mℓ (3 tablespoons) butter, melted
50 mℓ (3 tablespoons) cooking oil
15 mℓ (1 tablespoon) smooth apricot jam
1 clove garlic, crushed
15 mℓ (1 tablespoon) lemon juice

Mix together all the ingredients for the baste. Vlek the snoek (see page 11) and place it in an oiled hinged grid. Braai skin side down over low coals for about 25 minutes, basting frequently. Season with salt and pepper and serve immediately.
Serves 6

VARIATIONS
Apricot baste also goes well with kabeljou, kingklip and leervis.

Braaied snoek

Cape fish braai

1 yellowtail, about 1,5 kg, cleaned and
  gutted
1 clove garlic, cut into slivers

GARLIC AND WINE BASTE
75 mℓ (5 tablespoons) cooking oil
125 mℓ (½ cup) dry white wine
15 mℓ (1 tablespoon) lemon juice
5 mℓ (1 teaspoon) salt
freshly ground black pepper to taste
2 cloves garlic, crushed
5 mℓ (1 teaspoon) brown sugar

Mix together the ingredients for the baste.
Make several shallow incisions in the skin
of the yellowtail and place the garlic slivers
in them. Braai the fish in an oiled hinged
grid over low coals for about 20 minutes,
basting frequently. Serve immediately.
Serves 4 - 6

Above: Cape fish braai   *Below: Haarders in lemon marinade*

Haarders in lemon marinade

4 small whole haarders, cleaned and
  gutted

LEMON MARINADE
125 mℓ (½ cup) olive oil or cooking oil
60 mℓ (¼ cup) lemon juice
1 clove garlic, chopped
15 mℓ (1 tablespoon) freshly chopped or
  5 mℓ (1 teaspoon) dried oregano
30 mℓ (2 tablespoons) freshly chopped
  parsley
3 mℓ (a pinch) salt
freshly ground white pepper to taste

Mix together the ingredients for the marinade, pour it over the haarders and leave
them for 1½ hours. Braai the haarders in an
oiled hinged grid over low coals for 5 - 10
minutes, basting frequently with the marinade. Serve immediately.
Serves 4

VARIATIONS
Lemon marinade can also be used with
hake, galjoen, snoek or Cape salmon.

┌**HINT**─────────────────────
│ *As fish absorbs flavours more readily than*
│ *meat, it need be marinated for no longer than*
│ *2 hours.*
└─────────────────────────────

Fish which tend to be dry are excellent vlekked, seasoned with salt and pepper, and braaied with slices of tomato and onion.

Stumpnose with spicy tomato baste

2 stumpnose, cleaned and gutted

SPICY TOMATO BASTE
1 clove garlic, crushed
30 mℓ (2 tablespoons) chopped parsley
30 mℓ (2 tablespoons) tomato paste
125 mℓ (½ cup) wine vinegar
10 mℓ (2 teaspoons) lemon juice
5 mℓ (1 teaspoon) salt
freshly ground black pepper to taste
1 mℓ (a dash) cayenne pepper
1 mℓ (a dash) ground coriander

Mix together the ingredients for the baste. Make shallow incisions in the skin of the stumpnose and braai the fish in an oiled hinged grid or baskets over low coals for 15 - 20 minutes, basting frequently. Serve immediately.
Serves 6

VARIATIONS
Dageraad, John Dory, maasbanker, red roman, streepie, elf and zebra are all delicious braaied with this baste.

Kingklip with yoghurt sauce

4 large kingklip steaks, 250 g each
salt and freshly ground white pepper
  to taste
75 g (5 tablespoons) butter, melted

YOGHURT SAUCE
200 mℓ (¾ cup) natural yoghurt
50 mℓ (3 tablespoons) mayonnaise
30 mℓ (2 tablespoons) chopped parsley
3 mℓ (a pinch) freshly chopped or 1 mℓ
  (a dash) dried basil
salt and freshly ground black pepper
  to taste

Mix together the ingredients for the sauce and chill. Season the kingklip steaks, brush them with melted butter and braai them in an oiled hinged grid over moderate coals for 10 - 15 minutes. Serve the yoghurt sauce with the fish.
Serves 4

Kingklip with yoghurt sauce (centre), and Stumpnose (back) and elf with spicy tomato baste

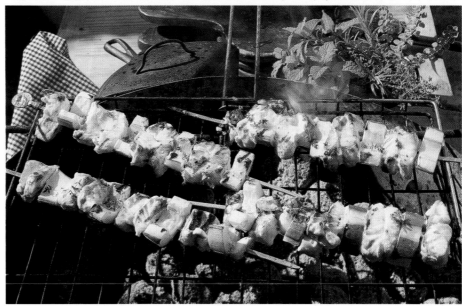

Cape salmon and cucumber kebabs

Cape salmon and cucumber kebabs

1 kg Cape salmon fillets
1 large English cucumber, halved
  lengthwise and seeded

WINE MARINADE
125 mℓ (½ cup) dry white wine
5 mℓ (1 teaspoon) sugar
60 g (¼ cup) butter, melted
30 mℓ (2 tablespoons) chopped fennel
  leaves or 15 mℓ (1 tablespoon)
  chopped dill
salt and freshly ground white pepper
  to taste

Cut the salmon into chunks. Mix together the ingredients for the marinade, pour it over the fish and refrigerate for 1 hour. Cut the cucumber into 25 mm slices. Thread pieces of salmon and cucumber alternately onto skewers and braai the kebabs over moderate coals until the fish is lightly browned, basting frequently with the marinade.
Serves 6

VARIATIONS
Kabeljou or yellowtail also braai well with cucumber on a skewer.

Kabeljou with vegetable stuffing

Kabeljou with vegetable stuffing

2 small kabeljou, cleaned and gutted
30 mℓ (2 tablespoons) cooking oil

VEGETABLE STUFFING
10 mℓ (2 teaspoons) butter, melted
½ green pepper, coarsely chopped
1 onion, coarsely chopped
1 tomato, peeled and coarsely chopped
1 clove garlic, crushed
5 mℓ (1 teaspoon) chopped parsley
5 mℓ (1 teaspoon) lemon juice
salt and freshly ground black pepper

Make 3 incisions lengthwise on each side of the kabeljou and brush the fish with cooking oil. Mix together the ingredients for the stuffing and spoon it into the incisions. Place each fish on a piece of foil, shiny side inside, and wrap well. Braai on a grid over moderate coals for 15-20 minutes or among the coals for about 10 minutes.
Serves 2

Trout with mushroom stuffing

6 whole trout, cleaned and gutted

MUSHROOM STUFFING
30 mℓ (2 tablespoons) butter
200 g mushrooms, coarsely chopped
250 g hake, finely chopped
5 mℓ (1 teaspoon) salt
freshly ground black pepper to taste
15 mℓ (1 tablespoon) chopped parsley
50 mℓ (3 tablespoons) cream
15 mℓ (1 tablespoon) lemon juice
5 mℓ (1 teaspoon) grated lemon rind

To make the stuffing, melt the butter in a pan or potjie, fry the mushrooms and add the hake, salt and pepper. Lift away from the heat, sprinkle the parsley over and mix in the cream, lemon juice and lemon rind. Spoon the stuffing into the belly cavity of the trout and secure with toothpicks or string. Braai over moderate coals for about 10 minutes. Serve immediately.
Serves 6

Grunter with creamy cheese stuffing

1 whole grunter, cleaned and gutted
250 mℓ (1 cup) Basic baste (page 12), using white wine

CREAMY CHEESE STUFFING
30 mℓ (2 tablespoons) butter
2 onions, chopped
250 mℓ (1 cup) fresh breadcrumbs
30 mℓ (2 tablespoons) chopped parsley
15 mℓ (1 tablespoon) lemon juice
salt and freshly ground black pepper to taste
15 mℓ (1 tablespoon) freshly chopped or 5 mℓ (1 teaspoon) dried thyme
125 mℓ (½ cup) cream
100 g Cheddar cheese, grated (250 mℓ)
2 potatoes, boiled and cut into cubes

To make the stuffing, melt the butter in a pan or potjie and fry the onion until it is translucent. Remove from the heat and mix in the remaining ingredients. Spoon the stuffing into the belly cavity of the grunter and secure with string or toothpicks. Braai in an oiled hinged grid or basket over moderate coals for about 20 minutes, basting frequently with the Basic baste.
Serves 4 - 6

HINT
A favourite fishermen's trick is to wrap whole, gutted fish in about 10 layers of newspaper, soak the parcel in sea water and bury it among the coals where it is left undisturbed for about 30 minutes. The blackened paper, together with the skin, is then peeled away, exposing the delicious, succulent flesh.

Red roman with caper sauce

1 whole red roman, cleaned and gutted

LEMON BASTE
125 mℓ (½ cup) cooking oil
60 mℓ (¼ cup) lemon juice
salt and freshly ground white pepper
to taste

CAPER SAUCE
50 mℓ (3 tablespoons) butter, melted
30 mℓ (2 tablespoons) freshly chopped or
10 mℓ (2 teaspoons) dried tarragon
30 mℓ (2 tablespoons) capers, coarsely
grated
5 mℓ (1 teaspoon) salt
freshly ground black pepper to taste

Mix together the ingredients for the lemon baste. Make the caper sauce by combining all the ingredients. Place the red roman in an oiled hinged grid or basket and braai over moderate coals for about 20 minutes, basting frequently. Serve the sauce with the red roman, straight off the grid.
Serves 2 - 4

Tunny with tomato sauce

1 kg tunny (about 4 slices)

TOMATO SAUCE
50 mℓ (3 tablespoons) cooking oil
1 large onion, chopped
2 cloves garlic, crushed
1 - 2 chillies, chopped
2 large tomatoes, peeled and coarsely
chopped
30 mℓ (2 tablespoons) tomato paste
75 mℓ (5 tablespoons) water
30 mℓ (2 tablespoons) wine vinegar
5 mℓ (1 teaspoon) lemon juice
salt and freshly ground black pepper

To make the sauce, heat the cooking oil in a potjie or on a skottel braai and fry the onion, garlic and chillies until the onion is translucent. Add the tomatoes and simmer until the mixture is pulpy. Stir in the remaining ingredients and simmer for another 10 minutes. Place each slice of tunny on the shiny side of a square of foil, spoon the sauce over and wrap securely. Cook the packets on a grid over moderate coals for about 20 minutes.
Serves 4

Above: Red roman with caper sauce   *Below: Tunny with tomato sauce*

Tasty sardines (back) and Angelfish with bacon

Angelfish with bacon

1 angelfish, filleted
75 m𝓁 (5 tablespoons) coarse salt
50 m𝓁 (3 tablespoons) butter, melted
15 m𝓁 (1 tablespoon) lemon juice
6 - 8 rashers rindless bacon

Place the angelfish in a flat dish, sprinkle coarse salt over and leave for about 30 minutes. Mix together the butter and lemon juice. Braai the fish skin down in an oiled hinged grid or basket over moderate coals for about 5 minutes. Turn and braai for another 5 minutes, basting all the while with the butter and lemon juice. Open the grid and place the bacon on the fillets. Braai until the bacon is cooked.
Serves 4

Tasty sardines

6 rashers lean rindless bacon
6 sardines

Wrap a rasher of bacon around each sardine and secure with a toothpick. Braai over moderate coals for about 5 minutes, turning once or twice. Serve immediately.
Serves 6

VARIATION
Sardine parcels: Place a sardine on a buttered piece of foil, sprinkle over lemon juice and season with salt and freshly ground black pepper. Wrap securely and braai over moderate coals for 5 minutes.

BRAAIING DIFFERENT KINDS OF FISH

The following fish are some of those most frequently caught in South African waters. Suggestions are given as to how best they can be braaied straight from the sea, without elaborate preparation. Unless otherwise indicated, a simple baste of 2 parts cooking oil to 1 part lemon juice, seasoned with salt and pepper, is ideal. A recipe for Tartare sauce to serve with the fish is given on page 87.

Angelfish
Cut into steaks or braai whole, or smoke.

Blacktail (Kolstert)
Braai fillets on the grid, basting with melted Mixed herb butter (page 89), or in well buttered foil.

Cape salmon (Geelbek)
Baste frequently with melted Lemon butter (page 89).

Elf (Shad)
Brush lightly with oil. Handle with care and braai as soon as possible after it was caught.

Fransmadam
This small fish must be braaied whole. Season with salt, pepper and lemon juice.

Grunter
Braai stuffed and baste well.

Gurnard
Brush with melted Mixed herb butter (page 89) and braai over moderate coals.

Haarder (Mullet)
Salt, wind-dry for about 2 hours, then braai over low coals.

Hottentot
Braai whole, basting well.

John Brown, John Dory
Brush frequently with a strongly herbed baste.

Kabeljou (Cob), Kingklip, Leervis
Braai in newspaper, with or without stuffing, or vlek open and baste well with melted Mixed herb butter (page 89).

Maasbanker, Mackerel
Salt and braai over low coals.

Marlin
Cut into steaks, season with salt, pepper and lemon juice. Braai quickly, taking care not to overcook.

Musselcracker (Biskop)
Braai in foil.

Red roman
Stuff and baste well.

Red (Yellow) steenbras
Remove liver, marinate, stuff and baste.

Seventy-four
Brush frequently with strongly herbed baste.

Streepie
Braai whole and baste well.

Tunny
Cut into steaks, marinate, brush with melted butter and baste well.

White steenbras, Yellowtail
Vlek open and baste well.

Herb mix

15 mℓ (1 tablespoon) each dried thyme,
  rosemary, summer savory, parsley and
  fennel
15 mℓ (1 tablespoon) dried grated orange
  rind
10 mℓ (2 teaspoons) ground bay leaves

Mix together all the ingredients and keep in
an airtight container. Sprinkle over any fish
to enhance its flavour.

Peri-peri prawns

4 - 6 large prawns, cleaned

PERI-PERI MARINADE
125 mℓ (½ cup) olive oil
30 mℓ (2 tablespoons) lemon juice
1 clove garlic, crushed
2 bay leaves
3 mℓ (a pinch) peri-peri
5 mℓ (1 teaspoon) ground cloves

Mix together the ingredients for the marinade, pour it over the prawns and leave for
2 hours. Braai the prawns over moderate
coals for about 6 minutes, basting frequently with the marinade. Serve immediately.
Serves 4 - 6

Perlemoen over the coals

4 perlemoen, cut horizontally into thin
  steaks
115 g (½ cup) melted butter
1 lemon, halved

Braai the perlemoen steaks over hot coals
for about 4 minutes. While the perlemoen is
cooking, stick a fork into the rind end of a
lemon half, dip the lemon into the melted
butter, then squeeze it over the perlemoen
to baste. When one lemon half is finished,
continue basting with the other. Turn the
steaks often. Serve the perlemoen as soon
as it is cooked or it will become rubbery.
Garlic butter (page 89) goes well with
perlemoen.
Serves 6

*Peri-peri prawns, Perlemoen over the coals and
Crayfish (see page 12)*

Spit-roasted pig

SPIT-ROASTING

For hundreds of years the problem of feeding a large crowd on high days and holidays was solved by spit-roasting a whole animal, and the operation itself became a focus of the celebration. Today, although whole carcases are no longer so easy to come by, a return to informality even in large gatherings has brought about renewed interest in spit-roasting, and it has become a popular method of catering for a considerable number of people.

With the correct equipment, spit-roasting carcases of lamb or pork presents little difficulty, but if you intend roasting a whole ox, because of the sheer size of the beast, it is advisable to call upon the services of a professional. Your butcher should be able to suggest how to contact one. As an alternative to roasting the whole animal, however, you may prefer to put whole cuts, such as prime rib, wing rib, sirloin, rump or buttock, on the spit or use combined cuts such as prime rib and wing rib, wing rib and sirloin, or sirloin and rump. Prime cuts such as these are not only easier to handle during cooking, but also easier to carve.

Perhaps to a greater degree than any other type of braai, a spit-roast has the potential to be a great success, or an absolute disaster. It requires perfect planning right from the purchase of the carcase to its serving – and plenty of time for the roasting!

THE EQUIPMENT
Spit-roasting may be done either with the carcase suspended over the coals on a horizontal spit which revolves to allow the meat to cook evenly, or on a cross spit which is stuck into the ground at an angle of 45°. The latter method, perfected in the Argentine and known as 'asado', requires that the carcase be split open and impaled on an iron rod with a cross-bar to which the hind legs of the beast are attached.

Manufactured spits are available in a number of different sizes but if you wish you can devise your own. For a horizontal spit you need a metal bar about 1,7 m long onto which the carcase can be secured. This bar should have two metal cross-pieces, each about 700 mm long, to which the forelegs and hind legs can be attached if the carcase is roasted open. Weld one of the cross-pieces onto the bar but leave the other loose so that the carcase can be placed in position on the spit before the forelegs are secured. The two uprights, also metal, should stand firmly in the ground, be sturdy enough to support the carcase-bearing rod, and allow adjustment of the height of the spit above the coals.

Both metal rods required for the asado spit should be flat rather than round, about 20 mm wide, and 7 mm thick. The cross-bar, about 700 mm long, is welded at right angles to the 1,7 m vertical rod 100 mm from one end. The other end is sharpened so that the rod sticks firmly into the ground. A metal hook, to which each hind shank of the carcase is fastened, is then welded to either end of the cross-bar. There is nothing worse than having your eagerly-awaited roast collapse into the fire just as it is almost ready, so be sure that your spit, whether asado or horizontal, is sturdy enough to bear the full weight of your beast.

THE FIRE
As with all braaiing, successful spit-roasting depends on a well-made fire. For information on the choice of fuel and building a fire, see page 7, remembering that the bed of coals required for spit-roasting must be considerably larger than that required for ordinary braaiing, and it must last a lot longer. Leadwood and ironwood make particularly good fuels as they burn for a long time and give off intense heat with little flame. A divided bed of coals is usually used for a horizontal spit-roast so that the heat is not concentrated on a relatively small area of the carcase. The bed should extend some 100 mm beyond either end of the carcase.

It is important that at least one additional fire is kept going to supply fresh coals throughout the roasting time, which will last for several hours.

THE CARCASE
The choice of the carcase is of utmost importance if you want tasty and tender meat. Old, heavy carcases not only take longer to cook than younger ones, but also turn out dry and tough. Make sure the one you select is that of a young, well-fed animal. For best results, the dressed weight of a lamb carcase should range between 10 and 20 kg. A 10 kg carcase feeds about 30 people, a 15 kg carcase about 40 people, and a 20 kg animal about 50 people. The most suitable weight for a pork carcase is between 13 and 18 kg. About 35 people can feed off a 13 kg beast, about 40 people off a 15 kg animal, and about 45 people off one weighing 18 kg.

Lamb and beef should be ordered a few days in advance so that the butcher has time to ripen the meat sufficiently. Ripening is regarded as the most effective method of tenderising meat since it is a natural process and not only results in tenderness, but also develops flavour. When purchasing a lamb carcase, ask the butcher to remove the head and neck, and the kidneys embedded in the suet. For an asado braai, however, leave the kidneys in place and let them roast with the rest of the carcase. Traditionally, they are offered to the guest of honour before the meat is served to the other guests. A pig's carcase should be left with the head and tail on. Remember to remove the kidneys, and cook them separately if you wish.

PREPARING THE CARCASE

Calculate the amount of salt and pepper required for seasoning the whole carcase by allowing 5 mℓ (1 teaspoon) salt and a pinch of freshly ground black pepper per kilogram. Mix the salt and pepper and rub a quarter of the mixture on the inside of the stomach cavity, keeping the rest to season the carcase towards the end of the cooking time. If the stomach cavity is to be closed, sprinkle inside it 45-75 mℓ (3-5 tablespoons) lemon juice to which coarsely chopped cloves of garlic or fresh rosemary may be added. The following mixture may also be used as a baste for lamb or to sprinkle inside either a lamb or a pork carcase:

50 mℓ (3 tablespoons) lemon juice
50 mℓ (3 tablespoons) orange juice
50 mℓ (3 tablespoons) cooking oil
5 - 6 cloves garlic, coarsely chopped
50 mℓ (3 tablespoons) coarse salt
10 mℓ (2 teaspoons) black pepper

SECURING THE CARCASE TO A HORIZONTAL SPIT

The animal can be attached to a horizontal spit in one of two ways: either 'wrapped around' (necessary if it has been stuffed) or with hind legs and forelegs splayed out. If you are using a manufactured spit, follow the instructions that usually come with it for securing the carcase. To stuff and 'wrap' your beast around a homemade spit, lay the carcase on its side and push the spit through the tail end, guiding it so that the point emerges through the mouth. Secure the spine of the carcase to the spit with thin wire. Spoon the stuffing into the stomach cavity, but not too tightly since it expands during cooking and may cause the cavity to burst open. To make removal of the stuffing easier, line the cavity with foil (dull side facing you) before packing in the stuffing. Sew up the cavity with a meat or trussing needle, making a few stitches at the tail end, and a few at the neck end. Then make individual stitches along the rest of the cavity at intervals of about 30 mm.

To keep the legs of the lamb or the pig's trotters out of the fire they must be secured to the spit. Loop a piece of thin stainless steel flexible wire around one of the hind feet, tighten the loop with pliers, then pass the wire around the other hind foot and pull it close to the first. Twist the two ends

SECURING A CARCASE TO A HORIZONTAL SPIT

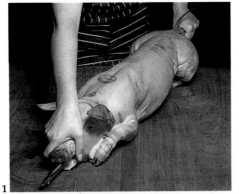

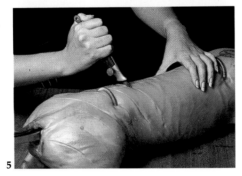

1. *To insert the spit, lay the carcase on its side and push the spit through from the tail end of the body to the mouth, making sure that the final position of the spit is as shown*

2. *Secure the spine to the spit with wire*

3. *Spoon the stuffing into the body cavity, taking care not to fill it too tightly*

4. *Sew up the cavity with a meat needle, placing stitches at the tail and the neck, and then at 30 mm intervals along the belly*

5. *Score the rind*

of wire together tightly and cut off any excess. Truss the forefeet in the same way. Then pull the hind feet close to the spit and secure them to it with wire. Do the same with the front feet.

To attach to a horizontal spit a lamb or pig that is to be splayed, first lay the carcase on its back and force the breast open. With a sharp cleaver or axe, chop just through the rib bones at the back bone. Force the ribs flat, then turn the carcase over and, starting at the tail end, insert the spit between the back bone and the layer of connective tissue and fat that covers it. Push the spit along the length of the carcase until it emerges through the middle of the neck or, in the case of a pig, through the mouth. Once the carcase is in position on the spit, secure the hind legs to the fixed cross-piece with wire. Move the adjustable cross-piece into position so that it will support the forelegs, fasten it securely to the spit, then attach the forelegs to it with wire.

Be sure to score the rind of a spit-roast pig, since it shrinks and cracks during the cooking process. Scoring also makes it easier to remove the crackling. Only dry seasoning should be used on the rind as the moisture content of a marinade or baste makes the crackling tough rather than crisp. Protect the ears and tail from scorching by covering them with foil.

OVER THE FIRE

Allow the fire to burn for 1-2 hours, until the coals are covered with white ash, before placing the spit and carcase in position. If possible, arrange the spit so that it is at a slight angle, with thicker parts of the carcase, such as the legs, nearer the coals. Although you may be eager to shorten the cooking time as much as possible, beware – it is important that the carcase does not roast too rapidly, as the outside becomes hard, preventing the heat from penetrating to the interior. Rather start the creature roasting 1 m above the coals and lower it to about 700 mm from the fire halfway through the cooking time. Thinner parts of the carcase should be protected with foil (shiny side out) once they are cooked.

Place a drip pan under the carcase so that dripping meat juices and fat may be collected and used for basting.

WHEN IS THE MEAT READY?

In spit-roasting, as in any form of braaiing, the length of time the meat must cook depends on a number of factors: the size of the carcase; the heat of the fire; prevailing wind and weather conditions; and, not least, the ability of the braaier to control both fire and meat. A 10 kg carcase takes about 2 hours, one of 15 kg about 3½ hours, and an 18 kg one about 5 hours to braai. When the animal has been cooking for the suggested length of time, insert a meat thermometer into the thickest part of the hind leg – it should register 65 °C for medium done and 70° C for well done meat. If a thermometer is not available, pierce the thickest part with a skewer. The juices should run clear, without any trace of pink.

CARVING THE CARCASE

Place the spit, complete with carcase, on a large table or giant-sized carving board and allow the meat to rest for 15 - 20 minutes before removing the spit. If the animal was stuffed, cut the string and open the belly, then remove the stuffing and serve slices of it separately. Steady the carcase with a carving fork and, using a sharp knife, first remove the larger cuts such as the legs and shoulders. Slice the meat of these joints thinly across the grain, starting from the shank end and carving around the bone with circular movements. To serve the loin and rib, make an incision parallel to the spine and along its length, then carve the meat crosswise into slices.

THE STUFFING

It is not necessary to stuff your animal (indeed, impossible if you use the asado method) but a tasty stuffing adds flavour to the meat and has the advantage of making it go further! The following stuffings are suitable for either lamb or pork:

Apple and herb stuffing

Rinse 10 apples, core them and cut them into wedges. Place the apple in the stomach cavity and add 250 mℓ (1 cup) chopped mint or a sprig of fresh rosemary or thyme.

Dried fruit stuffing

20 mℓ (1½ tablespoons) cooking oil
2 medium onions, chopped
1 clove garlic, chopped
1 kg minced pork or veal
500 g dried apricots, coarsely chopped
125 mℓ (½ cup) dry white wine
10 mℓ (2 teaspoons) grated lemon rind
125 mℓ (½ cup) chopped parsley
salt and freshly ground black pepper
**   to taste**

Heat the cooking oil in a pan and fry the onion and garlic gently until the onion is translucent. Add the remaining ingredients and mix lightly.

Pork and rice stuffing

3 kg minced pork
2 litres (8 cups) cooked rice
750 mℓ (3 cups) sultanas, soaked in hot
**   water or dry white wine, then drained**
3 - 4 cloves garlic, chopped
6 eggs, beaten
a dash cayenne pepper
salt and freshly ground black pepper
**   to taste**

Mix all the ingredients for the stuffing lightly but thoroughly.

HINT

Beef mince tends to be too dry for spit-roasting, so minced pork with a reasonable amount of fat is recommended.

Bread and wine stuffing

50 mℓ (3 tablespoons) cooking oil
3 onions, chopped
600 g mushrooms, chopped
2 litres (8 cups) fresh breadcrumbs
2 eggs, beaten
250 mℓ (1 cup) dry white wine
15 mℓ (1 tablespoon) freshly chopped or
**   5 mℓ (1 teaspoon) dried sage**
salt and freshly ground pepper

Heat the cooking oil in a pan and fry the onion and mushrooms gently until the onion is translucent. Add the remaining ingredients and mix well.

When you are spit-roasting a pig, very often the crackling is done to perfection while the rest of the meat requires further cooking. Simply remove the crackling and serve it as a snack, or keep it on one side and reheat it just before serving it with the pork.

ASADO

This Argentinian method of spit-roasting is becoming increasingly popular in South Africa, especially for roasting lamb. To prepare the carcase for an asado spit, force the breast open and, using a knife with a sharp point and a short, sturdy handle, cut just through the rib bones at the spine, leaving the meat intact. Apply pressure to the breast bones to snap the ribs so that they lie flat. Cut through the cartilage between the pelvic bones, then through the sinews around the ball joint of the leg and press the shank down so that the leg lies flat. Insert the spit at the tail end of the beast, between the back bone and the layer of fat and connective tissue that covers it, and guide the point gently with your hand so that it emerges through the middle of the neck. Slip the sinews of the shanks over the hooks on the cross-bar and fasten them with thin wire. Then cut open the thick layer of muscle on the leg so that it roasts more evenly, and fasten it to the cross-bar with wire. Green sticks can be used to open up the carcase even more (see photograph 8, opposite page).

Once the carcase is firmly in place, force the spit into the ground about 300 mm to one side of the fire and leaning over it at an angle of about 25° from the vertical. The weight of the carcase will bend it even further to an angle of about 45°. Roast the inside of the carcase first, arranging the coals so that the strongest heat is concentrated on the thicker areas, such as the leg. Then, about halfway through the cooking time, the spit must be pulled up, turned and reinserted into the ground so that the outside of the carcase can roast and the layer of fat covering it can cook to a crisp.

A lamb of 10 kg takes a total of about 3 hours to cook through, and one of 20 kg about 4 - 5 hours.

To give your asado lamb a truly Argentinian flavour, sprinkle Salmuera sauce on the inside of the carcase when it is cooked, and on the outside when the whole lamb is ready.

SECURING A CARCASE TO AN ASADO SPIT

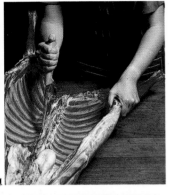 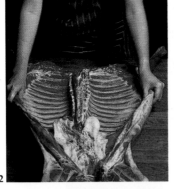  

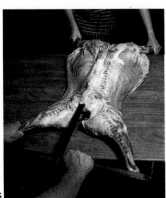   

1. *Cut through the rib bones at the spine, but not through the meat*
2. *Press the breast downwards so that the ribs snap and the carcase lies flat*
3. *Cut through the cartilage between the pelvic bones*
4. *Cut through the sinews around the ball joint*
5. *Insert the spit at the tail end between the back bone and the layer of fat and connective tissue, making sure it emerges through the middle of the neck*
6. *Slip the sinews of the shanks over the hooks on the cross-bar and fasten them with wire*
7. *Cut open the thick muscle layer of meat on the leg so that it roasts evenly*
8. *Use sharpened green sticks to hold the carcase open — lay the sticks across the back of the carcase and pierce the flesh on either side*
9. *Asado, braaiing the Argentinian way*

Salmuera sauce

125 mℓ (½ cup) coarse salt
75 mℓ (5 tablespoons) wine vinegar
1 large onion, coarsely chopped
3 - 5 cloves garlic, chopped
5 mℓ (1 teaspoon) Worcestershire sauce
30 mℓ (2 tablespoons) tomato purée
15 mℓ (1 tablespoon) pickling spice

Place all the ingredients in a 750 mℓ screw-top jar, fill it with boiling water and shake well. Let it stand for 1 hour, then top it up with boiling water if necessary. Make a few small holes in the top of the jar from which the sauce can be sprinkled.

Rib of mutton pot

POTJIEKOS

The old tradition of 'potjiekos' cooking has come to the fore again, as we discover what our grandparents have known all the time – that no other flavour can compare with a judicious combination of tasty meat morsels and fresh vegetables. Cooked long and slow, a potjiekos meal requires only the tastier, rather than the more expensive meat cuts, imaginative selection of vegetables that will blend well with the meat, slow-burning coals, and plenty of good conversation to while away the cooking time.

THE POT

Clean your new potjie (a three-legged iron cooking pot) thoroughly before attempting to cook in it. First scour the inside well to remove all particles of metal or rust. Fill it with water, add odd scraps of vegetables and vegetable peelings and let this 'soup' simmer away for at least an hour. Repeat the process four or five times. Alternatively, boil a mixture of vinegar and water in the pot several times. Rinse out the potjie and scour it thoroughly again, until the inside is as smooth as enamel – and don't forget the inside of the lid and the rim! Finally, grease the pot well with fat or cooking oil, both inside and out. To prevent it from rusting, always give the potjie a protective coating of cooking oil or fat before putting it away.

THE MEAT

Meat cuts that are not usually associated with the braai are ideal for potjiekos – the less tender cuts that are full of flavour, such as the neck, chuck, flat rib, brisket and shin of beef; the neck, shank and flank of lamb; and the shank, trotters and breast of pork. Delicacies such as oxtail, tripe, trotters and tongue lend their own unique flavours to a potjiekos dish, as do mutton and venison which are usually considered too tough to be braaied. These meats become beautifully tender in the long cooking process.

THE VEGETABLES

Choose firm, fresh vegetables or fruit, preferably those in season, whose flavour will blend well with the meat you are using.

THE FIRE

Potjiekos requires long, slow cooking over low heat, so keep the fire small. Add coals from a second fire from time to time to keep a constant temperature under the pot.

THE METHOD

Heat a mixture of cooking oil and butter (butter gives additional flavour) in a potjie over moderate coals. Cut the meat, chicken or fish into reasonably sized portions and brown them in the hot oil. A meat cut with a thick layer of fat, such as brisket, may be browned in its own fat. Remove some of the coals from under the pot, pour in some heated liquid, cover the pot tightly and let the meat simmer for an hour or two. Half an hour or so before the end of the cooking time add the vegetables in layers, those that take longest to cook (such as carrots and potatoes) first. You don't need to add much liquid as the tightly fitting lid traps the steam and the food cooks in its own juices. If you like a thicker sauce, add one or two potatoes right at the beginning of the cooking time so that they will cook to a pulp. The beauty of potjiekos is that it can safely be left to cook on its own – in fact, it is better left to cook on its own. Stir only at the beginning when the meat has been browned – and then leave well alone! As a general rule, a meat potjie requires 3 - 4 hours; a chicken potjie 2 - 3 hours; and a fish potjie about 1 hour cooking time.

Finally, to appreciate the potjiekos flavour, keep the side dishes simple – rice, pap or wholewheat bread and a crisp salad are all you need for a perfect meal.

Rib of mutton pot

1 kg rib of mutton, sawn into portions
1 green pepper
4 medium brinjals, sliced

TOMATO SAUCE
30 mℓ (2 tablespoons) cooking oil
1 onion, sliced
2 cloves garlic, crushed
1 x 410 g can tomatoes, drained and
  chopped
10 mℓ (2 teaspoons) salt
freshly ground black pepper to taste
1 sprig fresh rosemary
1 sprig fresh thyme
1 bay leaf
50 mℓ (3 tablespoons) chopped parsley

Braai the rib and the green pepper over hot coals until brown. Rub the skin off the green pepper, slice it and remove the seeds. To make the tomato sauce, heat the cooking oil in a potjie and fry the onion and garlic gently until the onion is translucent. Add the remaining ingredients and simmer for about 5 minutes. Pour the sauce out of the potjie, arrange the rib and brinjal and green pepper slices in layers in it and cover with the tomato sauce. Cover with a tightly fitting lid and simmer over low coals for about 3 hours, or until the meat is tender.
Serves 6

Waterblommetjie potjie

500 g breast or shin of mutton
15 mℓ (1 tablespoon) cooking oil
3 onions, sliced
5 mℓ (1 teaspoon) salt
freshly ground black pepper to taste
125 mℓ (½ cup) dry white wine
3 potatoes, peeled and cubed
1 kg fresh waterblommetjies or 2 x 410 g
  cans waterblommetjies
2 tomatoes, peeled and coarsely chopped

Cut the meat into portions. Heat the cooking oil in the potjie and brown the meat over moderate coals. Add the onion and fry gently until translucent. Season with salt and pepper. Heat the wine in a small pan, pour it over the meat, cover and simmer over low coals for about 2½ hours, until the meat is tender. Layer the potato, waterblommetjies and tomato on the meat, cover and simmer for another 30 minutes or until the vegetables are cooked.
Serves 6

Soutribbetjie pot (back) and Waterblommetjie potjie

Soutribbetjie pot

2 salted ribs of lamb or mutton
15 mℓ (1 tablespoon) cooking oil
500 mℓ (2 cups) meat stock
10 pickling onions
15 small carrots
3 medium potatoes, peeled and quartered
4 baby marrows, sliced thickly
15 mℓ (1 tablespoon) brown sugar
freshly ground black pepper to taste

Cut the ribs into portions. Heat the cooking oil in the potjie and brown the meat. Heat the meat stock in a small pan and add it to the potjie. Cover and let the meat simmer over moderate coals for about 3 hours, until it is tender. Layer the onions, carrots, potatoes and marrow on top of the meat, season with brown sugar and pepper, cover and leave to simmer for another 30 minutes until the vegetables are cooked.
Serves 8

HINT

To rid the soutribbetjie of excess salt, boil it first for about 30 minutes, then pat it dry with paper towel before browning it.

All-in-one pot

750 g bolo or boneless chuck of beef
1 pig's trotter
30 mℓ (2 tablespoons) cooking oil
2 onions, sliced
10 mℓ (2 teaspoons) salt
freshly ground black pepper to taste
200 g (250 mℓ/1 cup) uncooked pearl
  wheat
4 tomatoes, peeled and coarsely chopped
250 mℓ (1 cup) dry white wine
250 mℓ (1 cup) meat stock
2 leeks, sliced
5 baby marrows, sliced

Cut the bolo or chuck into cubes and saw the trotter into portions. Heat the cooking oil in a potjie and brown the meat. Add the onion and fry until it is translucent. Season with salt and pepper and add the pearl wheat and tomatoes. Heat the wine and meat stock together in a small pan over the fire, then pour the liquid into the potjie and cover with the lid. Let the meat simmer over low coals for 3 - 4 hours, until it is tender. Layer the leeks and baby marrows on top and simmer for another 20 minutes.
Serves 6 - 8

Tripe potjie with dumplings

Tripe potjie with dumplings

1 kg sheep's tripe, cleaned
15 mℓ (1 tablespoon) cooking oil
1 kg neck of mutton, cut into 20 mm
   slices
20 mℓ (1½ tablespoons) mild curry
   powder
375 mℓ (1½ cups) apple juice
375 mℓ (1½ cups) meat stock
20 mℓ (1½ tablespoons) salt
freshly ground black pepper to taste
15 mℓ (1 tablespoon) smooth apricot jam
10 pickling onions
12 small potatoes
250 mℓ (1 cup) dried apricots

DUMPLINGS
360 g (750 mℓ/3 cups) cake flour
10 mℓ (2 teaspoons) baking powder
7 mℓ (½ tablespoon) salt
30 mℓ (2 tablespoons) freshly chopped or
   10 mℓ (2 teaspoons) dried parsley
about 450 mℓ (1¾ cups) water

Rinse the tripe in cold water, pat dry, cut into cubes and set aside. Heat the cooking oil in a potjie and brown the mutton slices. Add the curry powder and fry gently. Heat together the apple juice and meat stock in a small pan, then pour the liquid into the potjie and add the tripe. Season with salt and pepper, then cover and simmer over moderate coals for 3 - 4 hours. While the tripe is cooking, make the dumpling mixture by sifting together the dry ingredients, adding the parsley and mixing well. Pour in enough water to mix to a soft dough. Set aside until the meat is almost tender. Add a little of the cooking liquid to the apricot jam and mix to a paste. Spoon this into the potjie, together with the vegetables and apricots. Finally, add the dumpling dough by dropping spoonfuls on top. Cover and simmer for another hour. Serve immediately.
Serves 8

HINT

Dumplings can be added to any of the potjiekos recipes.

Seafood potjie

15 mℓ (1 tablespoon) cooking oil
2 onions, sliced
2 cloves garlic, crushed
250 g smoked snoek, cut into cubes
250 g kingklip, cut into cubes
10 small potatoes
12 medium prawns, with shells
2 crayfish tails, with shells, cut into
   pieces
1 x 825 g can mussels, drained
15 mℓ (1 tablespoon) salt
freshly ground black pepper to taste
30 mℓ (2 tablespoons) lemon juice
50 mℓ (3 tablespoons) chopped parsley
4 lemon leaves, crushed
125 mℓ (½ cup) dry white wine

Heat the cooking oil in a potjie and fry the onion and garlic gently until the onion is translucent. Add the smoked snoek, king-klip, potatoes, prawns, crayfish tails and mussels in layers and season with salt and pepper. Sprinkle over the lemon juice and parsley and add the lemon leaves. Heat the wine in a small pan over the fire and pour it into the potjie. Cover and let the food simmer over low coals for 45 minutes. Serve immediately.
Serves 6

Allegaartjie potjie

500 g breast of pork, sawn into portions
500 g neck of mutton, sawn into 20 mm
   slices
500 g shin of beef, sawn into 20 mm
   slices
2 onions, quartered
2 turnips or parsnips, sliced
2 celery stalks, cut into chunks
6 carrots, sliced
2 tomatoes, peeled and quartered
1 green pepper, cut into strips
20 mℓ (1½ tablespoons) salt
freshly ground black pepper to taste
1 sprig fresh or 5 mℓ (1 teaspoon) dried
   rosemary
1 sprig fresh or 5 mℓ (1 teaspoon)
   dried dill
2 x 340 mℓ cans beer, heated
½ head cabbage, leaves separated

Brown the meat in a heated potjie. Add the onions and fry gently until they are translucent. Layer the vegetables, except the cabbage leaves, on the meat and season with salt, pepper and herbs. Pour the heated beer over, then arrange a layer of cabbage leaves on top. Cover and let simmer over moderate coals for 2 - 3 hours. Serve with pap (page 84).
Serves 6

HINTS

To separate the cabbage leaves, pour boiling water over the cabbage, then rinse it in cold water. It can then be opened and the leaves removed quite easily.

The meat can be allowed to simmer in the beer for 2 hours before the vegetables are added.

Allegaartjie potjie

Curry banana pot

30 mℓ (2 tablespoons) cooking oil
500 g minced beef
500 g minced pork
1 onion, chopped
1 clove garlic, crushed
30 mℓ (2 tablespoons) mild curry powder
125 mℓ (½ cup) meat stock
30 mℓ (2 tablespoons) smooth apricot jam
7 mℓ (½ tablespoon) salt
freshly ground black pepper to taste
1 x 410 g can whole tomatoes, drained
    and coarsely chopped
125 mℓ (½ cup) sultanas
4 bananas, sliced

Heat the cooking oil in the potjie and fry the meat over moderate coals until it changes colour. Add the onion and garlic and fry until the onion is translucent. Sprinkle the curry powder over and fry for a few minutes more. Heat the stock and apricot jam in a small saucepan and pour it over the meat. Season with salt and pepper, then add the tomatoes and sultanas, cover and simmer over low coals for about 1 hour. Add the bananas just before serving and reheat slightly.
Serves 6

Chicken potjie

15 mℓ (1 tablespoon) cooking oil
10 chicken thighs
2 onions, sliced
1 clove garlic, crushed
6 carrots, sliced
5 medium sweet potatoes, sliced
2 celery stalks, cut into chunks
250 g dried peaches
10 mℓ (2 teaspoons) salt
500 mℓ (2 cups) dry white wine
1 stick cinnamon
2 bay leaves
5 peppercorns

Heat the cooking oil in a potjie over moderate coals and brown the chicken thighs. Add the onion and garlic and fry until the onion is translucent. Layer the carrots, sweet potatoes, celery and dried peaches on top, and season with salt. Heat the wine, cinnamon, bay leaves and peppercorns together in a small pan over the fire and pour over the chicken and vegetables. Cover and simmer over low coals for 1 hour or until the chicken is tender. Check the amount of liquid in the pot from time to time and add more if necessary. Remove the cinnamon stick, bay leaves and peppercorns before serving.
Serves 8

Back to front: Venison potjie, Chicken potjie and Bean and pumpkin pot

Bean and pumpkin pot

6 rashers rindless bacon, chopped
1,5 kg beef flat rib, sawn into portions
1 large onion, coarsely chopped
10 mℓ (2 teaspoons) salt
freshly ground black pepper to taste
5 mℓ (1 teaspoon) grated nutmeg
2 bay leaves
125 mℓ (½ cup) dry red wine
125 mℓ (½ cup) meat stock
500 g green beans, shredded
600 g pumpkin, cut into cubes

Place the bacon in a potjie over hot coals and fry it in its own fat until crisp. Take out of the pot and put on one side. Brown the flat rib in the bacon fat, add the onion and fry until it is translucent. Season with salt, pepper and nutmeg and add the bay leaves. Heat together the wine and meat stock in a small pan and pour the liquid over the meat. Cover and simmer over low coals for about 3 hours, until the meat is nearly tender. Arrange the beans, pumpkin and bacon in layers on top of the meat and simmer for another 30 minutes until the vegetables are cooked. Remove the bay leaves before serving.
Serves 6

Rabbit potjie

1 rabbit, about 1,5 kg
15 mℓ (1 tablespoon) cooking oil
15 mℓ (1 tablespoon) butter
3 onions, sliced
300 g button mushrooms
12 small potatoes
300 g carrots, cut into strips
300 g green beans, halved
125 mℓ (½ cup) chutney
60 mℓ (¼ cup) cream
60 mℓ (¼ cup) mayonnaise
125 mℓ (½ cup) chicken stock
1 packet brown onion soup powder
freshly ground black pepper to taste
100 g Cheddar cheese, grated (250 mℓ)

Cut the rabbit into portions. Heat together the cooking oil and butter in a potjie and brown the rabbit portions. Add the onion and mushrooms and fry until the onion is translucent. Layer the potatoes, carrots and green beans on top of the meat. Mix together the remaining ingredients except the cheese and pour over the meat and vegetables. Cover and simmer over low coals for 1-2 hours, until the meat is tender. Sprinkle the cheese over before serving.
Serves 6

VARIATION
Chicken portions can be used instead of rabbit.

Venison potjie

2 kg boneless venison, cut into cubes
    (kudu or rooibok is excellent)
2 kg shin of beef, sliced
75 mℓ (5 tablespoons) cake flour
15 mℓ (1 tablespoon) salt
freshly ground black pepper to taste
3 mℓ (a pinch) grated nutmeg
3 mℓ (a pinch) ground cloves
1 x 410 g can mushroom soup
1 litre (4 cups) apple juice
250 mℓ (1 cup) dry white wine
4 potatoes, cut into cubes
5 carrots, sliced
4 onions, sliced
1 butternut, sliced
4 tomatoes, peeled and coarsely chopped

DUMPLINGS
360 g (750 mℓ/3 cups) self-raising flour
7 mℓ (½ tablespoon) salt
about 375 mℓ (1½ cups) milk

Brown the meat in a heated potjie, then add the flour, seasonings and soup. Heat together the apple juice and wine in a small pan and pour over the meat. Cover and simmer over low coals for 3-4 hours. Layer the vegetables on top of the meat, cover and simmer for another half hour, until the meat is tender. Prepare the dumplings by mixing all the ingredients to a soft dough. Spoon the dough on top of the vegetables, cover and keep tightly closed while it cooks for another 30 minutes. Serve immediately.
Serves 10-12

Let potjiekos cook undisturbed, only checking occasionally that there is enough liquid. If necessary, add a little heated wine or stock to the pot.

Above and below right: Stir-fry braai

STIR-FRY ON THE SKOTTEL

'Stir-fry braaiing' came to South Africa relatively recently under the guise of the 'Mongolian' or 'Chinese' braai and quickly proved its popularity as a means of entertaining. With good reason – it is easy to prepare, quick to cook and it encourages guest participation. In fact, if the guests don't participate, they don't eat!

A selection of meat, fish and vegetables is stir-fried on a skottel braai and a sauce is added when the other ingredients are almost cooked. Because the cooking time is very short, the meat should be tender and the vegetables fresh and young. Cut both meat and vegetables into thin strips, slices or small cubes and arrange them attractively and colourfully to tempt your guests, with the sauces arrayed nearby. Then sit back and let everyone choose their own food and cook it.

Garlic sauce

250 mℓ (1 cup) natural yoghurt
125 mℓ (½ cup) dry white wine
6 cloves garlic, chopped
salt and freshly ground black pepper

Combine all the ingredients.
Makes 375 mℓ

Sweet and sour sauce

250 mℓ (1 cup) pineapple juice
2 mℓ (a pinch) ground ginger
15 mℓ (1 tablespoon) soy sauce
30 mℓ (2 tablespoons) wine vinegar
20 mℓ (1½ tablespoons) brown sugar
30 mℓ (2 tablespoons) cornflour

Combine all the ingredients.
Makes 300 mℓ

Herb sauce

125 mℓ (½ cup) dry white wine
10 mℓ (2 teaspoons) tomato paste
5 mℓ (1 teaspoon) brown sugar
5 mℓ (1 teaspoon) soy sauce
15 mℓ (1 tablespoon) freshly chopped
    herbs (rosemary, marjoram, parsley) or
    5 mℓ (1 teaspoon) dried mixed herbs

Combine all the ingredients.
Makes 125 mℓ

Chilli sauce

15 mℓ (1 tablespoon) soy sauce
15 mℓ (1 tablespoon) brown sugar
5 mℓ (1 teaspoon) chilli sauce
10 mℓ (2 teaspoons) cornflour
50 mℓ (3 tablespoons) meat stock

Mix together the soy sauce, brown sugar and chilli sauce. Make a paste of the cornflour and a little of the meat stock. Add the remaining meat stock and stir until smooth. Add the soy sauce mixture and mix well.
Makes 50 mℓ

Barbecue sauce

20 mℓ (1½ tablespoons) tomato sauce
15 mℓ (1 tablespoon) Worcestershire sauce
15 mℓ (1 tablespoon) vinegar
15 mℓ (1 tablespoon) brown sugar
5 mℓ (1 teaspoon) prepared mustard

Combine all the ingredients.
Makes 50 mℓ

Stir-fry braai

300 g rump steak, cut into strips
300 g boned thick rib of lamb, cut
    into strips
125 g Vienna sausages, sliced
125 g frankfurters, sliced
2 chicken breasts, cut into strips
2 large onions, sliced thinly
1 green pepper, cut into strips
3 carrots, cut into strips
200 g spinach leaves, shredded
300 g mushrooms, sliced
½ cauliflower, broken into small pieces
200 g broccoli, broken into small pieces
1 x 410 g can whole kernel corn, drained
1 x 410 g can pineapple chunks, drained
    and liquid reserved for Sweet and sour
    sauce
1 x 190 g can shrimps, drained
salt and freshly ground black pepper
    to taste

Arrange the ingredients attractively in separate groups on a large tray or in individual dishes. Heat a skottel braai and add a little cooking oil so that the surface is evenly greased. Brown the meat first, then add the vegetables in the order given. Fry for a few minutes, stirring all the time. When the food is almost cooked add a sauce of your choice and the shrimps. Stir-fry the meat and vegetables for a few minutes longer. Season with salt and pepper and serve immediately with boiled rice.
Serves 10

VARIATIONS
Any combination of vegetables can be served. Try also leeks, spring onions, celery, bean sprouts, brinjal, frozen green beans, red or yellow pepper, canned asparagus, baby marrows or bamboo shoots.

HINT
Once cooked, stir-fry dishes should be eaten immediately, while the vegetables are still crisp.

Fillet (left) and lamb for Eastern fondue and Lamb fondue

FONDUE OVER THE COALS

Cooking a fondue over the coals makes an interesting change from an ordinary braai, and ensures the participation of all your guests.

Any cut of beef, lamb or pork that is suitable for braaiing can be used for fondue. Allowing about 250 g per person, cut the meat into chunks large enough to be securely pierced by a fondue fork or skewer but small enough to cook reasonably quickly. Small pork sausages, smoked sausages or cubes of liver or kidney may be added to give variety. Dry the meat thoroughly before cooking it to prevent the oil from spattering.

Fill a small potjie (¼, ½ or ¾ size) half to three-quarters full with cooking oil and heat the oil until a cube of bread dropped into it browns in 60 seconds. Once the oil is hot, remove some coals so that the fire is low, as the pot retains heat for a long time.

Now everyone can begin cooking his own meat and, when it is ready, can dip it into a sauce of his own choice. Serve the sauces chilled so that they cool the meat slightly for eating.

Make a sauce over the coals in a ½ or ¾ size potjie and keep it warm at the edge of the fire while you are braaiing the meat.

Lamb fondue

1,5 kg boneless leg or shoulder of lamb, cut into 20 mm cubes
1 litre (4 cups) cooking oil

FONDUE MARINADE
30 mℓ (2 tablespoons) vinegar
60 mℓ (¼ cup) cooking oil
60 mℓ (¼ cup) meat stock
1 clove garlic, crushed
1 leek or onion, sliced
15 mℓ (1 tablespoon) freshly chopped or
  5 mℓ (1 teaspoon) dried rosemary
freshly ground black pepper to taste

Mix together all the marinade ingredients and marinate the meat for 2-3 hours. Remove the meat from the marinade and pat it dry with paper towel. Heat the cooking oil in a potjie and keep it warm over low coals. Skewer a cube of meat onto a fondue fork and let the meat cook in the oil for about 2 minutes. Serve with a variety of sauces, bread and a crisp salad.
Serves 6

Eastern fondue

1,5 kg fillet of veal, pork or beef

MEAT STOCK
15 mℓ (1 tablespoon) butter
2 onions, finely chopped
1 clove garlic, crushed
250 mℓ (1 cup) dry white wine
1 litre (4 cups) meat stock
30 mℓ (2 tablespoons) medium cream sherry
freshly ground black pepper to taste

To make the meat stock, melt the butter in a potjie over moderate coals and fry the onion and garlic until the onion is translucent. Add the remaining ingredients and simmer for 5 minutes. Keep the meat stock hot over a low fire. Slice the meat paper thin and thread each slice onto a skewer. Dip the meat into the piping hot stock for 3 minutes, then into a savoury sauce. Serve with fresh bread.
Serves 6

Apricot dip

15 mℓ (1 tablespoon) cooking oil
1 onion, chopped
1 x 410 g can apricots, drained and
 chopped
salt and freshly ground black pepper
 to taste
15 mℓ (1 tablespoon) chopped root ginger
10 mℓ (2 teaspoons) cornflour

Heat the cooking oil in a potjie and fry the onion until it is translucent. Add the apricots, seasoning and ginger and simmer for 5 minutes. Thicken the sauce with cornflour mixed to a paste with water and simmer for another 5 minutes. Cool before serving.
Makes 250 mℓ

VARIATION
Pineapple dip: Use crushed pineapple instead of apricots.

Creamy chutney dip

250 mℓ (1 cup) cream cheese
30 mℓ (2 tablespoons) chutney
15 mℓ (1 tablespoon) lemon juice
10 mℓ (2 teaspoons) tomato sauce
75 mℓ (5 tablespoons) cream

Mix together all the ingredients and blend well. Serve chilled.
Makes 375 mℓ

Mustard sauce

200 mℓ (¾ cup) evaporated milk
50 mℓ (3 tablespoons) dry mustard
1 onion, chopped
10 mℓ (2 teaspoons) sugar
3 mℓ (a pinch) salt

Mix together all the ingredients and blend well. Serve chilled.
Makes 200 mℓ

Tomato sauce

10 mℓ (2 teaspoons) cooking oil
1 onion, chopped
1 green pepper, chopped
1 clove garlic, crushed
1 x 410 g can tomato soup
500 mℓ (2 cups) meat stock
30 mℓ (2 tablespoons) brown sugar
freshly ground black pepper to taste

Clockwise from top right: Tomato sauce, Creamy chutney dip, Apricot dip, Curry sauce, Chapatis and Mustard sauce

Heat the cooking oil in a potjie and fry the onion, green pepper and garlic until the onion is translucent. Add the soup and meat stock and bring to the boil. Then add the sugar and pepper and simmer for a few minutes. Chill before serving.
Makes 750 mℓ

Curry sauce

15 mℓ (1 tablespoon) cooking oil
4 chives or 1 small onion, finely chopped
5 mℓ (1 teaspoon) curry powder
125 mℓ (½ cup) mayonnaise
15 mℓ (1 tablespoon) apricot jam
1 mℓ (a dash) salt
10 mℓ (2 teaspoons) lemon juice or vinegar

Heat the cooking oil in a potjie and fry the chives or onion gently. Add the curry powder and fry for a few minutes. Remove from the heat, add the remaining ingredients and mix well. Chill before serving.
Makes 125 mℓ

Chapatis

260 g (500 mℓ/2 cups) wholewheat flour
5 mℓ (1 teaspoon) salt
about 200 mℓ (¾ cup) water
cooking oil for frying

Mix together the flour and salt and add enough water to mix to a stiff dough. Knead the dough well until it is firm and elastic, then leave it for 30 minutes. Shape it into a roll and divide it evenly into 12 pieces. Roll out each piece paper thin. Heat the cooking oil in a large frying pan and, just before serving, fry each chapati for 1 minute on each side. Drain on paper towel.
Makes 12

HINT
Although usually eaten with curry, chapatis are also an excellent accompaniment to a fondue.

PAELLA

This traditional Spanish dish gains a wonderful smoky flavour when it is cooked over an open wood fire. If you don't have the true paella pan — a large flat pan with two handles — a large shallow saucepan or a skottel braai can be used just as effectively.

Paella

30 ml (2 tablespoons) olive oil
30 ml (2 tablespoons) cooking oil
10 chicken thighs
1 large onion, chopped
3 cloves garlic, chopped
1 green pepper, sliced
300 g button mushrooms
600 g (750 ml/3 cups) rice
15 ml (1 tablespoon) salt
freshly ground black pepper to taste
5 ml (1 teaspoon) saffron dissolved in
    30 ml (2 tablespoons) chicken stock
2 litres (8 cups) fish or chicken stock,
    heated
½ chorizo sausage, sliced thinly
500 g cocktail sausages
10 large prawns
20 black mussels or mussels in brine
300 g frozen peas
15 black olives
1 x 410 g can tomatoes, drained and
    chopped

Heat the olive oil and cooking oil in the pan over moderate coals. Fry the chicken thighs until they are golden brown, then add the onion, garlic, green pepper and mushrooms and fry them until the onion is translucent. Add the rice, seasoning, saffron and stock and simmer for 45 minutes, or until the chicken and rice are cooked. Arrange the slices of chorizo sausage, the cocktail sausages, prawns, mussels, peas, olives and tomato on top and simmer for another 10 minutes, adding more stock if necessary.
Serves 10

---HINTS---

Always use a shallow saucepan as the rice will cook to a pulp at the bottom of a deep one.

The secret of a good paella is to use a concentrated fish stock, for which you need:
  1 kg fish heads, bones and unwanted
    trimmings
  1 onion
  1 leek
  1 bouquet garni
  3 white peppercorns
  2 litres (8 cups) water
Combine all the ingredients and bring slowly to the boil, skimming off any scum as it rises. Cover, leaving the lid slightly open, and simmer for 30 minutes. Strain the stock without pressing the fish and vegetables against the sieve. Cool and refrigerate or freeze.

Springbok sosaties

2 kg leg of springbok, cut into cubes
200 g speck, cut into cubes

SOSATIE MARINADE
15 mℓ (1 tablespoon) cooking oil
2 large onions, sliced
30 mℓ (2 tablespoons) curry powder
15 mℓ (1 tablespoon) smooth apricot jam
15 mℓ (1 tablespoon) cake flour
500 mℓ (2 cups) vinegar
5 mℓ (1 teaspoon) salt
3 bay leaves
freshly ground black pepper to taste

To prepare the marinade, heat the cooking oil in a saucepan and fry the onion until it is translucent. Sprinkle the curry powder over and fry gently, stirring. Add the remaining ingredients and simmer for about 5 minutes. Allow to cool. Thread the springbok and speck cubes alternately onto wooden skewers, place in a dish and pour the marinade over. Marinate the sosaties overnight or longer, turning them occasionally. Braai over low coals for about 15 minutes, until they are cooked as desired. Heat the marinade and serve it with the sosaties.
Serves 6 - 8

VARIATION
Springbok and apricot sosaties: Thread dried apricots and pickling onions alternately with the meat onto the skewers.

Kudu fillet in sour cream marinade

1 whole kudu fillet
salt and freshly ground black pepper

SOUR CREAM MARINADE
250 mℓ (1 cup) sour cream
15 mℓ (1 tablespoon) lemon juice
5 mℓ (1 teaspoon) grated lemon rind
30 mℓ (2 tablespoons) freshly chopped
    herbs (thyme, marjoram, basil) or
    10 mℓ (2 teaspoons) dried mixed herbs
salt and freshly ground white pepper

Mix together all the marinade ingredients and marinate the fillet overnight. Braai it over moderate to hot coals for about 30 minutes, basting frequently with the marinade. Carve the meat across the grain and season to taste with salt and pepper.
Serves 6 - 8

VENISON

Venison at any time is a special treat, and venison on the braai is really something different. Like any other red meat, it should come from a young, well-fed animal and be well ripened. Because it does tend to be dry and tough, most cuts benefit from long, slow cooking in a potjie. Fillet, however, is the exception and can be braaied successfully. If you do braai other cuts, be generous with marinades, bastes and sauces to keep the meat moist. Spices that blend particularly well with venison are juniper berries, cloves, nutmeg, bay leaves, coriander and allspice.

Braaied warthog rib

1 warthog rib

CURRY MARINADE
20 mℓ (1½ tablespoons) cooking oil
4 large onions, chopped
1 small chilli, seeded and finely chopped
30 mℓ (2 tablespoons) curry powder
30 mℓ (2 tablespoons) brown sugar
5 mℓ (1 teaspoon) salt
5 mℓ (1 teaspoon) turmeric
30 mℓ (2 tablespoons) smooth apricot jam
500 mℓ (2 cups) dry white wine or vinegar

To make the marinade, heat the cooking oil in a pan and fry the onion until it is translucent. Add the chilli and curry powder and fry gently. Add the remaining ingredients and simmer for about 5 minutes. Allow the marinade to cool, then leave the meat in it overnight. Remove the meat and pat dry with paper towel. Braai the rib over low coals for about 30 minutes, basting frequently with the marinade.
Serves 6 - 8

VARIATIONS
Springbok, kudu or rooibok can be used.

Springbok sosaties (back), Kudu fillet in sour cream marinade (left) and Braaied warthog rib

SNACKS

The aroma of food cooking over coals is enough to send anyone's taste buds drooling, and a few snacks are a good idea to keep the hunger pangs at bay until the main meal is ready.

Mini kebabs and Bacon rolls

Chicken liver snack (left) and Mixed seafood packet

Mini kebabs

1 leg of lamb, boned and cut into 15 mm cubes
500 g dried apricots
250 g dried apple rings
salt and freshly ground black pepper to taste

ROSEMARY MARINADE
500 mℓ (2 cups) Basic marinade (page 12), using white wine
15 mℓ (1 tablespoon) freshly chopped or 5 mℓ (1 teaspoon) dried rosemary

Thread 2 cubes of lamb, 2 apricots and 2 apple rings alternately onto small wooden skewers. Mix together the ingredients for the marinade and marinate the kebabs overnight in the refrigerator. Remove from the marinade and pat dry with paper towel. Braai the kebabs over moderate coals for about 10 minutes, basting frequently with the marinade. Season with salt and pepper.
Makes 20 kebabs

VARIATIONS
Fish kebabs: Thread onto each small wooden skewer a cube of hake, tomato, green pepper, bacon and a pickling onion. Marinate the kebabs in 500 mℓ (2 cups) Basic marinade (page 12), using orange juice instead of wine and adding oregano and parsley.

Kidney kebabs: Thread onto each small wooden skewer a cube of lamb or ox kidney, a mushroom and a cherry tomato. Marinate the kebabs in Basic marinade (page 12) to which oregano has been added.

Banana kebabs: Thread 2 cubes of Russian sausage and 2 banana chunks onto each small wooden skewer. While braaiing baste with a mixture of 50 mℓ (3 tablespoons) honey, 30 mℓ (2 tablespoons) lemon juice and 2 mℓ (a pinch) ground ginger.

Fruit kebabs: Thread cubes of pineapple, banana and kiwi fruit and a whole strawberry onto each small wooden skewer. Braai for 5 minutes, basting with a mixture of 2 parts orange juice, 1 part honey and 1 part rum.

Bacon rolls

Wrap a rasher of bacon around any of the following combinations and secure with a toothpick:

- **firm figs sprinkled with lemon juice**
- **slices of Russian sausage or frankfurter and chunks of banana, with mustard**
- **chunks of frankfurter and Cheddar cheese**
- **chicken livers and stoned prunes**
- **peaches or apricots (fresh or dried)**
- **cubes of lamb's liver seasoned with black pepper, and pineapple chunks**

Braai the bacon rolls over moderate coals for about 10 minutes.

Chicken liver snack

30 m*ℓ* **(2 tablespoons) cooking oil**
500 g chicken livers, cleaned
1 onion, coarsely chopped
1 clove garlic, chopped
1 apple, grated
**10 m*ℓ* (2 teaspoons) freshly chopped or
  3 m*ℓ* (a pinch) dried thyme**
**salt and freshly ground black pepper
  to taste**
4 slices bread, crusts removed
butter for spreading

Heat the cooking oil in a potjie or heavy-based pan or on a skottel braai and fry the chicken livers, stirring constantly, until they change colour. Add the onion and garlic and fry until the onion is translucent. Stir in the apple, thyme and seasoning and fry for another 2 - 3 minutes, stirring constantly. Toast 4 slices of bread over the coals and butter them. Serve the chicken livers on the toast.
Serves 4

Tuna spread

1 x 200 g can tuna, drained
125 m*ℓ* (½ cup) smooth cottage cheese
**30 m*ℓ* (2 tablespoons) chopped capers or
  gherkins**
freshly ground black pepper to taste
30 m*ℓ* (2 tablespoons) mayonnaise
15 m*ℓ* (1 tablespoon) lemon juice

Flake the tuna lightly. Thoroughly mix the remaining ingredients and add to the tuna. Spoon into a large bowl or individual dishes and chill well. Serve with wholewheat bread or savoury biscuits.
Serves 6

VARIATIONS
Smoked hake, smoked snoek or shredded biltong can be used instead of the tuna.

Mixed seafood packet

**300 g kingklip, filleted and cut into strips
  or cubes**
250 g fresh or frozen calamari, sliced
125 g prawns, shelled
**30 m*ℓ* (2 tablespoons) freshly chopped or
  10 m*ℓ* (2 teaspoons) dried dill**
7 m*ℓ* (½ tablespoon) salt
freshly ground black pepper to taste
50 m*ℓ* (3 tablespoons) lemon juice
75 m*ℓ* (5 tablespoons) cream
**20 m*ℓ* (1½ tablespoons) medium cream
  sherry**
2 m*ℓ* (a pinch) paprika
30 m*ℓ* (2 tablespoons) butter

Combine all the ingredients and divide the mixture into 6 equal portions. Place each portion on a greased piece of foil, shiny side up, and wrap well. Braai over moderate coals for 10 - 15 minutes.
Serves 6

Dipped vegetables

500 g carrots, cut into strips
½ cauliflower, broken into pieces
250 g baby marrows, sliced thickly

APPLE DIP
1 green apple, peeled and grated
175 m*ℓ* (¾ cup) cream cheese
15 m*ℓ* (1 tablespoon) lemon juice
125 m*ℓ* (½ cup) cream, whipped
1 m*ℓ* (a dash) paprika
**15 m*ℓ* (1 tablespoon) freshly chopped dill
  or 5 m*ℓ* (1 teaspoon) dried mixed herbs**

To make the dip, mix together the apple, cream cheese and lemon juice. Fold in the cream and add the paprika and dill. Serve with the fresh, crisp vegetables.
Serves 6

Tuna spread (left) and Dipped vegetables

Pearl wheat salad (back) and Rice salad with peaches

Pearl wheat salad

30 mℓ (2 tablespoons) sugar
2 sticks cinnamon
5 mℓ (1 teaspoon) turmeric
15 mℓ (1 tablespoon) ground coriander
5 mℓ (1 teaspoon) salt
1 litre (4 cups) water
200 g (250 mℓ/1 cup) pearl wheat
125 mℓ (½ cup) mayonnaise
6 gherkins, chopped
1 x 410 g can peaches, drained and coarsely chopped
125 mℓ (½ cup) seedless raisins (optional)

Add the sugar, cinnamon sticks, turmeric, coriander and salt to the water and bring to the boil. Pour in the pearl wheat, return to the boil and simmer for 1 hour until the wheat is soft. Drain, remove the cinnamon sticks and allow to cool. Gently mix the wheat and the remaining ingredients and chill before serving.
Serves 8

Rice salad with peaches

1 x 410 g can peach slices, drained
½ green pepper, finely chopped
75 mℓ (5 tablespoons) chopped walnuts
  (optional)
3 gherkins, chopped
500 mℓ (2 cups) cooked rice
125 mℓ (½ cup) natural yoghurt
125 mℓ (½ cup) mayonnaise
5 mℓ (1 teaspoon) salt
freshly ground black pepper to taste
15 mℓ (1 tablespoon) freshly chopped
  parsley

Mix together the peaches, green pepper, walnuts and gherkins. Add the rice and stir in lightly. Combine the yoghurt, mayonnaise, salt and pepper and add to the salad. Sprinkle with parsley and chill.
Serves 8

SALADS

Cool and crisp, salads are the perfect foil to succulent meat straight off the braai. With the wide variety of fresh ingredients to choose from, tempting salads can be created throughout the year just by using what is available at its peak of freshness. And the joy of salads at a braai is that they can be made in advance, kept in the refrigerator and a dressing added just before serving.

---HINT---

Rice salad can be prepared the day before, covered with cling wrap and kept in the refrigerator. Almost any combination of ingredients can be added to the rice, but avoid those such as tomato and cucumber which tend to draw moisture and make the salad soggy.

Mixed bean salad

1 x 410 g can green beans, drained
1 x 410 g can baked beans in tomato sauce
1 x 410 g can butter beans, drained
1 green pepper, chopped (optional)
2 onions, chopped
250 mℓ (1 cup) sultanas
125 mℓ (½ cup) brown sugar
50 mℓ (3 tablespoons) cooking oil
125 mℓ (½ cup) vinegar
100 mℓ (6 tablespoons) water
freshly ground black pepper to taste

Mix together the beans, green pepper, onion and sultanas and set aside. Heat together the brown sugar, oil, vinegar, water and pepper, bring to the boil and simmer, stirring, until the sugar has dissolved. Allow to cool, then pour over the bean mixture.
Serves 8 - 10

┌─*HINT*────────────────────────
│ *This salad is best made at least 2 days in advance to allow the flavour to develop.*
└────────────────────────────────

Green salad with bean sprouts

1 head lettuce, washed and torn into pieces
1 green pepper, cut into strips
1 avocado, stoned, peeled and sliced
½ English cucumber, sliced
2 celery stalks, sliced
125 mℓ (½ cup) bean sprouts
75 mℓ (5 tablespoons) Basic French dressing (page 74)
125 mℓ (½ cup) croutons (see Crunchy cheese and pineapple salad, page 76)
50 g Feta cheese, cut into cubes

In a bowl mix together the salad ingredients except the croutons and cheese. Pour the French dressing over just before serving and toss the salad gently. Sprinkle the croutons and cheese on top.
Serves 6 - 8

┌─*HINT*────────────────────────
│ *Make a cucumber salad by slicing a cucumber and pouring a dressing of natural yoghurt, salt, freshly ground pepper and chopped fresh mint over. Cucumber tends to draw moisture, so prepare the salad no longer than 2 hours in advance.*
└────────────────────────────────

Mixed bean salad (back) and Curried beans

Green salad with bean sprouts

Curried beans

30 mℓ (2 tablespoons) cooking oil
3 onions, sliced
30 mℓ (2 tablespoons) medium curry powder
5 mℓ (1 teaspoon) turmeric
30 mℓ (2 tablespoons) cornflour
500 g green beans, sliced and parcooked
200 mℓ (¾ cup) sugar
5 mℓ (1 teaspoon) salt
250 mℓ (1 cup) vinegar
400 mℓ (1½ cups) sultanas

Heat the cooking oil in a saucepan and fry the onion gently until it is translucent. Stir in the curry powder, turmeric and cornflour and fry for 1 minute longer. Add the remaining ingredients and simmer for 15 minutes. Allow to cool, then chill before serving.
Serves 8

Sweet and sour carrots

1 kg carrots, sliced
1 green pepper, cut into strips
2 onions, sliced
250 ml (1 cup) tomato purée
200 ml (¾ cup) white vinegar
50 ml (3 tablespoons) cooking oil
10 ml (2 teaspoons) Worcestershire sauce
250 ml (1 cup) sugar
5 ml (1 teaspoon) prepared mustard
5 ml (1 teaspoon) salt
freshly ground black pepper to taste

Boil the carrots until they are cooked but still firm, then drain. Arrange the carrots, green pepper and onion slices in layers in a bowl with a lid, ending with a layer of carrots. Mix together the remaining ingredients in a saucepan, bring to the boil and simmer for 2 minutes, stirring constantly. Pour the sauce over the salad, allow to cool, then marinate, covered, in the refrigerator for 2 days.
Serves 8 - 10

Spanspek and cheese salad

½ head lettuce, washed and torn into pieces
½ spanspek, other melon or pawpaw, scooped into balls
2 apples, cut into cubes
100 g Cheddar cheese, cut into cubes
4 smoked sausages, sliced
30 ml (2 tablespoons) freshly chopped parsley

MAYONNAISE DRESSING
75 ml (5 tablespoons) mayonnaise
75 ml (5 tablespoons) cream
15 ml (1 tablespoon) freshly chopped or
  5 ml (1 teaspoon) dried mint

Line a salad bowl with the lettuce leaves. Arrange the spanspek, apple, cheese and sausage on top and sprinkle with parsley. Combine the ingredients for the dressing and serve it with the salad.
Serves 6

HINT

Try a salad of raw mushrooms and baby marrow and onion slices in a dressing of mashed avocado mixed with equal quantities of cream and mayonnaise and seasoned with salt and pepper.

Basic French dressing

250 ml (1 cup) olive oil or cooking oil
125 ml (½ cup) wine vinegar or lemon juice
1 clove garlic, crushed
3 ml (a pinch) dry mustard
salt and freshly ground black pepper

Combine all the ingredients in a jar and shake well.
Makes 375 ml

VARIATION
The garlic and mustard can be omitted or substituted with finely chopped onion and herbs of your choice.

Left to right: Sweet and sour carrots, Coleslaw, Spanspek and cheese salad, Spinach and avocado salad and Potato salad with apple and bacon

Potato salad with apple and bacon

1 kg potatoes
100 g rindless bacon, coarsely chopped
5 chives, finely chopped
30 mℓ (2 tablespoons) capers
50 mℓ (3 tablespoons) chopped parsley
5 mℓ (1 teaspoon) salt
freshly ground black pepper to taste
125 mℓ (½ cup) mayonnaise
125 mℓ (½ cup) sour cream
2 green apples
15 mℓ (1 tablespoon) lemon juice

Boil the potatoes in their jackets for about 25 minutes until they are tender, then peel and cube them. Fry the bacon until crisp and add it to the potatoes. Add the remaining ingredients except the apples and lemon juice and mix gently. The salad can be prepared in advance to this stage and kept in the refrigerator. To continue, cut the unpeeled apples into thin wedges and sprinkle the lemon juice over. Stir the apples gently into the potato mixture.
Serves 10

VARIATIONS
Other attractive garnishes for potato salad are: chopped celery, cucumber, green or red pepper, gherkin, hard-boiled egg and black or green olives.

Spinach and avocado salad

250 g young spinach leaves
2 avocados, stoned, peeled and sliced
8 bacon rashers, finely chopped and fried crisp
100 mℓ (6 tablespoons) flaked almonds
75 mℓ (5 tablespoons) Basic French dressing (page 74)

Pour boiling water over the spinach leaves, leave for 2 seconds, then drain. Refresh the leaves in cold water, pat them dry and line a salad bowl with them. Arrange the avocado slices on the leaves and sprinkle the bacon and almonds over. Shake the dressing well and add it to the salad just before serving.
Serves 8

Coleslaw

¼ head cabbage, finely shredded
4 bananas, sliced
1 avocado, stoned, peeled and cut into cubes
125 mℓ (½ cup) sultanas, soaked in orange juice, then drained

CONDENSED MILK DRESSING
1 x 225 g can condensed milk
50 mℓ (3 tablespoons) white vinegar
30 mℓ (2 tablespoons) cooking oil
5 mℓ (1 teaspoon) French mustard
5 mℓ (1 teaspoon) salt
white pepper to taste

Lightly mix together the salad ingredients in a bowl. Beat together the dressing ingredients and pour the dressing over the salad.
Serves 8

VARIATION
Instead of the Condensed milk dressing, you can use a dressing made up of 250 mℓ (1 cup) mayonnaise mixed with 30 mℓ (2 tablespoons) lemon juice.

Spicy peach salad

1 x 825 g can cling peaches, drained
1 x 250 g can apple rings or 2 apples, cored and sliced (optional)
2 onions, chopped
5 mℓ (1 teaspoon) mixed spice
2 whole cloves
5 mℓ (1 teaspoon) turmeric
5 mℓ (1 teaspoon) curry powder
3 mℓ (a pinch) ground coriander
3 mℓ (a pinch) salt
1 mℓ (a dash) cayenne pepper
250 mℓ (1 cup) sugar
125 mℓ (½ cup) white vinegar
30 mℓ (2 tablespoons) cornflour

In a saucepan mix together all the ingredients except the cornflour. Bring the mixture to the boil and let it simmer for 15 minutes. Make a smooth paste of the cornflour and a little water and stir it into the sauce to thicken it. Allow the salad to cool and chill before serving.
Serves 6

VARIATION
Use 500 g fresh peaches, stoned and halved, or 500 g dried peaches, soaked in 250 mℓ (1 cup) orange juice, instead of the canned peaches.

Spiked dried fruit salad

500 mℓ (2 cups) weak tea
250 mℓ (1 cup) brandy, rum or gin
5 mℓ (1 teaspoon) grated orange or lemon rind
2 sticks cinnamon
2 whole cloves
50 mℓ (3 tablespoons) sugar
250 g prunes
250 g dried apple rings
250 g dried apricots

In a saucepan mix together all the ingredients except the dried fruit. Bring to the boil and simmer, stirring, until the sugar has dissolved. Remove the cinnamon sticks and cloves. Pack layers of fruit in sterilised glass jars and pour the warm liquid over. Allow to cool, then seal the jars. Store the fruit salad for 6 weeks to let all the flavours blend thoroughly.
Serves 8

VARIATION
Marinate 500 g mixed dried fruit overnight in 250 mℓ (1 cup) orange juice. Drain the fruit, stir in 125 mℓ (½ cup) granadilla yoghurt and serve immediately.

Onions in herb mustard sauce

1 kg pickling onions, cooked

HERB MUSTARD SAUCE
75 mℓ (5 tablespoons) sugar
salt to taste
10 mℓ (2 teaspoons) dry mustard
2 eggs, beaten
125 mℓ (½ cup) white vinegar
15 mℓ (1 tablespoon) freshly chopped herbs (dill, oregano) or 5 mℓ (1 teaspoon) dried mixed herbs
5 mℓ (1 teaspoon) Pommery mustard or 5 mℓ (1 teaspoon) crushed mustard seed
125 mℓ (½ cup) cream

To make the sauce, mix together the sugar, salt and dry mustard, add to the eggs in the top of a double boiler or heatproof basin and beat well. Add the vinegar slowly and stir over boiling water until the mixture thickens. Cool and add the herbs and mustard. Just before serving add the cream, then pour the sauce over the onions.
Serves 6 - 8

┌─ *HINT* ─────────────────
│ *The sauce, minus the cream, can be made in advance and kept in the refrigerator until required. Stir in the cream just before serving with the onions.*
└──────────────────────────

Clockwise from top right: Spiked dried fruit salad, Onions in herb mustard sauce and Spicy peach salad

Crunchy cheese and pineapple salad

½ loaf white bread, crust removed
cooking oil for frying
1 head butter lettuce, torn into pieces
50 g Cheddar cheese, cut into cubes
1 x 410 g can pineapple chunks, drained
1 onion, chopped
6 gherkins, chopped
125 mℓ (½ cup) Condensed milk dressing (see Coleslaw, page 75)

Make croutons by cutting the bread into 10 mm cubes, frying them in heated cooking oil until they are golden brown, then draining them on paper towel. Arrange the lettuce in a bowl and add the croutons and remaining ingredients. Pour the dressing over the salad just before serving.
Serves 6

VARIATION
Mustard sauce (page 87) can be used instead of the Condensed milk dressing.

Savoury samp

240 g (300 mℓ/1¼ cups) samp
1 litre (4 cups) water
375 mℓ (1½ cups) milk
30 mℓ (2 tablespoons) cooking oil
2 onions, chopped
2 green peppers, chopped
250 g bacon, finely chopped
3 tomatoes, peeled and chopped
5 mℓ (1 teaspoon) dry mustard
3 mℓ (a pinch) cayenne pepper
5 mℓ (1 teaspoon) salt
freshly ground black pepper to taste
3 eggs, beaten
200 g Cheddar cheese, grated (500 mℓ)

Soak the samp in the water overnight, then bring it to the boil and simmer for 4 hours, adding more water if necessary during the cooking time. Add the milk and simmer for another 20 minutes. Heat the cooking oil in a potjie and fry the onion, green pepper and bacon until the onion is translucent. Add the tomatoes, mustard, cayenne pepper and seasoning and simmer for 5 minutes. Spoon the cooked samp into the vegetable mixture, mix it in and fold in the eggs. Sprinkle the grated cheese on top and leave the potjie in a warm place near the fire for about 30 minutes, until the samp has set.
Serves 8 - 10

Pumpkin pot

15 mℓ (1 tablespoon) cooking oil
2 onions, sliced
500 g pumpkin, peeled and sliced
250 g dried peaches
250 mℓ (1 cup) boiling water
10 mℓ (2 teaspoons) salt
freshly ground black pepper to taste
1 stick cinnamon
50 mℓ (3 tablespoons) brown sugar
50 mℓ (3 tablespoons) butter

Heat the cooking oil in a potjie and fry the onion slices until they are translucent. Add the pumpkin slices and dried peaches in layers, then the boiling water, seasoning and cinnamon. Cover and cook gently over low coals for about 30 minutes. Take off the lid and simmer for another 10 minutes until the liquid is reduced. Add the brown sugar and the butter and cook until the sugar has melted. Remove the cinnamon stick and serve hot.
Serves 6

VEGETABLES

Vegetables cooked in foil among the coals or skewered and braaied directly over the fire make popular braai accompaniments – and deservedly so, for they need minimum preparation yet are full of flavour. With the aid of a potjie, however, more adventurous vegetable dishes can be concocted and some interesting flavour combinations achieved.

Cheesy sweetcorn

300 mℓ (1¼ cups) milk
30 mℓ (2 tablespoons) butter
3 eggs, separated
1 x 410 g can whole kernel sweetcorn or 250 mℓ (1 cup) fresh mealie kernels
100 g Cheddar cheese, grated (250 mℓ)
5 mℓ (1 teaspoon) French mustard
250 mℓ (1 cup) fresh breadcrumbs
salt and freshly ground black pepper

Heat together the milk and butter in a potjie. Beat the egg yolks and stir into the milk together with the remaining ingredients except the egg whites. Whisk the egg whites and fold them in lightly. Cover and allow to cook gently over low coals for about 30 minutes, until set.
Serves 6

Back to front: Cheesy sweetcorn, Pumpkin pot and Savoury samp

Ratatouille

Creamy potato and mushroom bake (back) and Fruity sweet potato

Ratatouille

30 mℓ (2 tablespoons) cooking oil
1 onion, sliced
1 clove garlic, crushed
1 brinjal, cut into cubes
1 green pepper, seeded and cut into strips
250 g baby marrows, sliced
1 x 410 g can whole tomatoes or 5 fresh
    tomatoes, peeled and chopped
5 mℓ (1 teaspoon) brown sugar
freshly ground black pepper to taste
5 mℓ (1 teaspoon) salt
7 mℓ (½ tablespoon) freshly chopped or
    2 mℓ (a pinch) dried basil

Heat the cooking oil in a potjie or heavy-based pan, or on a skottel braai. Fry the onion and garlic until the onion is translucent, then add the brinjal, green pepper and baby marrow and fry for a few minutes longer. Add the remaining ingredients and simmer over moderate heat for about 10 minutes, until the vegetables are tender.
Serves 6

---HINT---
Choose fresh, firm vegetables that will keep their texture and colour without cooking to a pulp.

Creamy potato and mushroom bake

6 medium potatoes, cooked in their skins
300 g mushrooms, sliced
2 tomatoes, peeled and chopped
2 onions, sliced
3 mℓ (a pinch) salt
2 mℓ (a pinch) nutmeg
15 mℓ (1 tablespoon) freshly chopped or
    5 mℓ (1 teaspoon) dried parsley
250 mℓ (1 cup) cream
50 g Cheddar cheese, grated (125 mℓ)

Skin the potatoes and slice them thickly. Arrange the potato slices, the mushrooms, tomatoes and onion in layers in a potjie and sprinkle over the salt, nutmeg and parsley. Stir in the cream and scatter cheese over. Cook over low coals for about 30 minutes.
Serves 6

VARIATION
Stir in 1 packet of cream of chicken soup mixed with 125 mℓ (½ cup) milk when adding the cream.

Fruity sweet potato

500 g sweet potatoes, cooked whole, then
    peeled and sliced
2 bananas, sliced
2 apples, cored and sliced
50 mℓ (3 tablespoons) butter, melted
50 mℓ (3 tablespoons) brown sugar or
    honey
50 mℓ (3 tablespoons) orange juice
salt to taste

Arrange the sweet potato, banana and apple slices in layers in a potjie. Mix together the remaining ingredients and pour the liquid over the layers. Cook gently at the edge of the braai over moderate coals for about 20 minutes.
Serves 6

VARIATION
Sprinkle crushed ginger nuts over to add a delicious flavour.

Vegetables in foil

Carrots, mealies, mushrooms, potatoes, onions, sweet potatoes, baby marrows, butternut, even asparagus – all these can be braaied successfully in foil

Just wash the vegetables thoroughly and place each one, still wet, on a piece of foil (the moisture steams the vegetable inside the foil packet). Sprinkle over salt and pepper, or any other seasoning of your choice, and add a dollop of butter or Garlic butter (page 89) before closing the packet and wrapping securely. Try cooking some of the smaller vegetables, such as pickling onions, mushrooms and baby marrows, together and letting their flavours mingle. Nestle potatoes, onions and sweet potatoes among the coals for about 45 minutes and let other vegetables cook on the grid for about 30 minutes.

Vegetables in foil (back) and Stuffed vegetables

Stuffed vegetables

potatoes, cooked and halved lengthwise
butternut, cooked, halved lengthwise and seeds removed
green peppers, parcooked, stem end and seeds removed
baby marrows, parcooked and halved lengthwise
tomatoes, stalk ends removed, brushed with melted butter
brown mushrooms, stalk removed, brushed with melted butter

CHEESE STUFFING
100 g Cheddar cheese, grated (250 mℓ)
250 mℓ (1 cup) fresh breadcrumbs
1 small onion, finely chopped
15 mℓ (1 tablespoon) freshly chopped or 5 mℓ (1 teaspoon) dried parsley
salt and freshly ground black pepper to taste
30 mℓ (2 tablespoons) butter, melted
50 mℓ (3 tablespoons) milk
a little extra grated cheese

Mix together the ingredients for the stuffing. Scoop out the flesh of the potatoes and mix it with some of the stuffing. Do the same with the butternut, baby marrows and tomatoes, keeping the stuffing for each vegetable separate. Spoon the stuffing into the vegetables and sprinkle extra grated cheese over. Wrap the vegetables in foil again or arrange in a heatproof dish and cover. Heat through on low coals until the cheese has melted.

Vegetables on a skewer

Vegetables on a skewer

cucumber, sliced thickly or cut into chunks
brinjal, cut into cubes
mushrooms, whole or cut into chunks
red or green pepper, seeded and cut into chunks
tomatoes, whole or quartered
baby marrows, sliced thickly
pickling onions, parcooked
Basic marinade (page 12), using white wine

Choose a combination of the above vegetables, aiming for complementary colours and flavours. Marinate the vegetable pieces in the Basic marinade for several hours, then thread them onto skewers. Braai the skewered vegetables over moderate coals for about 10 minutes, turning occasionally and basting with the marinade.

VARIATION
For a touch of sweetness, add chunks of fruit such as pineapple or banana.

Back to front: Stokbrood, Roosterkoek, Potbrood and Askoek

BREADS

'B read' in the context of 'braai' takes on a whole range of new meanings — it can be a traditionally South African 'cook-over-the-coals' bread such as 'roosterkoek' or 'potbrood', any of a wide variety of home-made loaves from the kitchen, or a shop-bought French loaf revitalised with herb butter and heated on the fire. However it may be presented, bread is always a firm favourite at any braai.

Basic ready-mix

1 kg (2 litres/8 cups) white or brown
   bread flour
30 mℓ (2 tablespoons) baking powder
125 mℓ (½ cup) skim milk powder
10 mℓ (2 teaspoons) salt
250 g (about 1 cup) butter

Combine all the dry ingredients. Cut the butter into small pieces and rub it into the dry ingredients with your fingertips. This mixture can be stored in an airtight container in a cool dry place for up to 2 months.
Makes 2,5 litres

Roosterkoek in a jiffy

1 litre Basic ready-mix
2 eggs
150 mℓ water

Place the Basic ready-mix in a large bowl. Beat together the eggs and water and add to the Basic ready-mix, mixing well. Knead into a firm, elastic dough. Shape the dough into 6 cakes and braai them on a grid over low coals for about 20 minutes.
Makes 6 cakes

VARIATIONS
Askoek: Add 225 mℓ water to 1 litre Basic ready-mix and knead to a dough. Shape into 6 cakes and wrap each in greased foil, leaving space for the dough to expand. Bake directly among moderate coals for about 15 minutes.

Potbrood: Beat together 2 eggs and 325 mℓ buttermilk, and add to 2 litres Basic ready-mix. Knead to a dough. Shape the dough into a ball and place it in a greased, flat cast-iron pot, leaving room for expansion. Place the pot among moderate coals, putting a few coals on the lid. Bake the potbrood for about 45 minutes, or until done.

Stokbrood: Add 200 mℓ water to 1 litre Basic ready-mix and knead to a dough. Tear off a piece of dough, roll it into a thin 'sausage' and wrap the sausage around a stick. Braai over moderate coals for 20 minutes.

---HINT---
These recipes are useful if you are in a hurry. Use the yeast dough given in the Potbrood recipe (page 82) to make traditional roosterkoek, askoek and stokbrood.

Cheesy mealie bread

480 g (1 litre/4 cups) self-raising flour
3 mℓ (a pinch) salt
50 mℓ (3 tablespoons) sugar
30 mℓ (2 tablespoons) cooking oil
2 eggs, beaten
200 mℓ (¾ cup) milk or evaporated milk
1 x 410 g can cream-style sweetcorn
100 g Cheddar cheese, grated (250 mℓ)
15 mℓ (1 tablespoon) freshly chopped
    parsley

Mix the flour, salt and sugar. Beat together
the oil, eggs and milk and add to the flour
mixture. Add the remaining ingredients,
mix thoroughly and spoon the dough into
a well-greased, flat cast-iron pot. Make a
hollow in the ground, line it with moderate
coals and place the pot on top. Place a few
coals on the lid and bake for about 1 hour.
Alternatively, spoon the dough into a large,
greased cocoa can or boston loaf pan, cover
and let it bake on the grid over moderate
coals for about 2 hours. The bread can also
be baked in a greased loaf pan at 180 °C for
1 hour or microwaved at 70% power for 12
minutes.
Makes 1 loaf

VARIATION
Bacon bread: Chop and fry 4 rashers rindless bacon and use instead of the sugar.

Fruit bread

1 egg, beaten
500 mℓ (2 cups) natural yoghurt
260 g (500 mℓ/2 cups) wholewheat flour
180 g (250 mℓ/1 cup) oats
60 g (125 mℓ/½ cup) cake flour
75 mℓ (5 tablespoons) sunflower seeds
250 mℓ (1 cup) seedless raisins
15 mℓ (1 tablespoon) salt
7 mℓ (½ tablespoon) bicarbonate of soda
1 apple, grated

Beat together the egg and yoghurt, then
mix the remaining ingredients and stir in
the egg and yoghurt. Spoon the dough into
a greased foil tart pan, cover with another
tart pan and fasten together with wet
clothes pegs. Braai on a grid over moderate
coals for 1 hour, turning frequently. Alternatively, bake in a greased loaf pan at 180 °C
for 1 hour or microwave at 70% power for 12
minutes.
Makes 1 loaf

Back to front: Cheesy mealie bread, Easy wholewheat bread and Fruit bread

Easy wholewheat bread

360 g (690 mℓ/2¾ cups) Nutty Wheat
160 g (250 mℓ/1 cup) sesame seeds or bran
5 mℓ (1 teaspoon) salt
5 mℓ (1 teaspoon) bicarbonate of soda
500 mℓ (2 cups) buttermilk or natural
    yoghurt, or 310 mℓ (1¼ cups) milk
50 mℓ (3 tablespoons) honey
15 mℓ (1 tablespoon) peanut butter
    (optional)

Mix together the dry ingredients, reserving
some of the sesame seeds or bran to sprinkle over the loaf. Combine the buttermilk,
honey and peanut butter, add to the dry ingredients and mix thoroughly. Spoon the
dough into a greased 230 mm foil tart pan
and sprinkle the sesame seeds or bran over.
Invert another tart pan over the first and
fasten the two together with wet clothes
pegs. Braai on a grid over moderate coals for
45 minutes, turning frequently. Alternatively, bake in a greased loaf pan at 190 °C
for 1¼ hours or microwave at 70% power for
12 minutes.
Makes 1 loaf

VARIATION
Substitute crushed wheat or wholewheat
flour for half the Nutty Wheat.

Herby cottage cheese rolls

480 g (1 litre/4 cups) self-raising flour
5 mℓ (1 teaspoon) salt
1 onion, chopped
10 mℓ (2 teaspoons) freshly chopped
   herbs (thyme, oregano, marjoram) or
   3 mℓ (a pinch) dried mixed herbs
freshly ground black pepper to taste
250 mℓ (1 cup) smooth cottage cheese
200 mℓ (¾ cup) milk
1 egg, beaten

Sift together the flour and salt and add the onion, herbs and pepper. Combine the cottage cheese, milk and egg, add and mix thoroughly. Shape the mixture into about 8 balls and arrange in a greased round cake pan. Brush with beaten egg and bake at 180 °C for 1¼ hours. Serve hot.
Makes 8 rolls

VARIATION

'Croissants': Divide the dough into thirds and roll each one into a circle. Cut each circle into 8 wedges and, starting at the wide end, roll up each wedge and bend it into a crescent shape. Sprinkle with cheese and bake at 200 °C for 12 minutes. Alternatively, microwave 8 at a time at 100% power for 4 minutes.

Potbrood

15 mℓ (1 tablespoon) yeast granules or
   1 yeast cake
10 mℓ (2 teaspoons) sugar
250 mℓ (1 cup) lukewarm water
1,2 kg (2,5 litres/10 cups) white bread
   flour
10 mℓ (2 teaspoons) salt
100 g (250 mℓ/1 cup) rolled oats
15 mℓ (1 tablespoon) cooking oil
about 500 mℓ (2 cups) lukewarm water

Mix together the yeast, sugar, water and 30 mℓ (2 tablespoons) of the flour, and leave in a warm place for 10 minutes. Sift together the remaining flour and salt and add the oats and then the yeast mixture and oil. Pour in the extra 500 mℓ (2 cups) water little by little to make a fairly stiff dough. Knead it well and allow to rise until double in size. Knead the dough again, shape it into a round and place it in a well-greased, flat cast-iron pot. Cover and leave to rise again near the coals. Make a hollow in the ground, line it with moderate coals and rest

Clockwise from top right: Garlic and herb French loaf, Herby cottage cheese rolls, Pumpkin bread, Toasted sandwiches, Beer bread, Pearl wheat vetkoek and Potbrood

the pot on top. Place a few coals on the lid to ensure even heat distribution and bake for about 1 hour or until done.
Makes 1 loaf

---HINTS---

If you use instant yeast, mix 15 mℓ (1 table-spoon) instant yeast with the dry ingredients and then add the oil and 750 mℓ (3 cups) water.

Knead the dough until it is smooth and elastic, but be careful not to knead it too much.

If possible, prepare a yeast bread a day ahead. Knead it, cover it with cling wrap and leave it to rise in the refrigerator overnight. Cold dough which rises slowly gives a better texture and will stay fresh longer.

Pearl wheat vetkoek

240 g (500 mℓ/2 cups) cake flour
10 mℓ (2 teaspoons) baking powder
5 mℓ (1 teaspoon) salt
500 mℓ (2 cups) cooked pearl wheat
2 eggs, beaten
150 mℓ milk
15 mℓ (1 tablespoon) butter, melted
cooking oil for frying

Sift together the dry ingredients and add the pearl wheat. Combine the eggs, milk and melted butter and add to the dry ingredients, mixing thoroughly. Shape the dough into flat cakes. Heat the cooking oil in a potjie over hot coals and deep-fry the cakes until they are golden brown. Drain on paper towel and serve with butter and honey.
Makes 8 cakes

bottom crust. Spread the butter mixture between the slices, then wrap the loaf in foil and place directly among moderate coals for 25 minutes. Alternatively, bake in a preheated oven at 200 °C for 25 minutes.
Makes 1 loaf

VARIATION
Use any of the butters on page 89.

Beer bread

480 g (1 litre/4 cups) self-raising flour
1 x 340 mℓ can beer
3 mℓ (a pinch) salt

Mix together all the ingredients and spoon the dough into a greased foil tart pan. Cover with another tart pan, fasten with wet clothes pegs and braai on the grid over hot coals for about 1 hour, turning frequently. Alternatively, bake in a greased loaf pan at 180 °C for 1 hour or microwave in a ring mould at 70% power for 10 minutes.
Makes 1 loaf

VARIATIONS
Cheese bread: Omit the beer and add 500 mℓ (2 cups) buttermilk, 150 g Cheddar cheese, grated (375 mℓ), and 1 crushed clove garlic.

Onion bread: Omit the beer and add 500 mℓ (2 cups) buttermilk and 1 packet onion soup mix.

Herb bread: Omit the beer and add 500 mℓ (2 cups) buttermilk, 5 mℓ (1 teaspoon) oregano and 5 mℓ (1 teaspoon) marjoram. Sprinkle some grated cheese and dry mustard on the dough before baking.

Pumpkin bread

420 g (875 mℓ/3½ cups) cake flour
5 mℓ (1 teaspoon) baking powder
10 mℓ (2 teaspoons) bicarbonate of soda
7 mℓ (½ tablespoon) salt
5 mℓ (1 teaspoon) ground cinnamon
125 mℓ (½ cup) chopped nuts (optional)
200 mℓ (¾ cup) seedless raisins (optional)
170 g (¾ cup) butter
375 mℓ (1½ cups) sugar
4 eggs
500 g cooked pumpkin, drained
200 mℓ (¾ cup) water

Sift together the flour, baking powder, bicarbonate of soda, salt and cinnamon and add the nuts and raisins. In another bowl, cream the butter and sugar and add the eggs one by one, beating well after each addition. Add the pumpkin, then the dry ingredients and water alternately. Mix thoroughly. Spoon the mixture into 2 well-greased loaf pans and bake at 180 °C for

1 hour. Alternatively, microwave each loaf at 70% power for 10 minutes.
Makes 2 loaves

Garlic and herb French loaf

1 long French loaf

GARLIC AND HERB BUTTER
180 g (¾ cup) butter
2 cloves garlic, finely chopped
3 mℓ (½ teaspoon) French mustard
30 mℓ (2 tablespoons) freshly chopped
** parsley**
3 mℓ (a pinch) freshly chopped thyme
30 mℓ (2 tablespoons) finely chopped
** onion**
freshly ground black pepper to taste

Beat the butter until it is soft, add the remaining ingredients and mix well. Slice the bread thickly without cutting through the

Toasted sandwiches

Make a sandwich using any of the following fillings and braai in a hinged grid until golden brown.

FILLINGS
cheese, tomato and onion
cooked chicken and mayonnaise
onion, bacon, green pepper and tomato
savoury mince
banana, ham, cheese and garlic
banana with ground cinnamon and sugar
minced lamb's liver, with onion and
** tomato slices**

PAP

'Pap' (a kind of porridge made with mealie meal) distinguishes a South African braai from any other barbecue. In fact, if you are eating firm 'stywepap' you are probably in the Transvaal, whereas if you are served the more crumbly 'krummelpap' or 'putupap', chances are you are braaiing in the Orange Free State or Natal – although such regional differences are no longer as strong as they used to be. A sauce into which the pap is dipped is generally served with it.

Krummelpap

750 mℓ (3 cups) water
10 mℓ (2 teaspoons) salt
600 g (1 litre/4 cups) mealie meal

Bring the water and salt to the boil in a potjie over hot coals. Pour in the mealie meal to form a cone in the centre of the potjie but do not stir. Reduce the heat by removing some coals, put the lid on the potjie and let the pap simmer for 5 minutes, until a skin forms. Stir with a fork until the pap is fine and crumbly. Cover again and let the pap simmer for another 45 minutes.
Serves 6

Stywepap (back) and Krummelpap, with Tomato sauce

Stywepap

1 litre (4 cups) water
10 mℓ (2 teaspoons) salt
30 mℓ (2 tablespoons) butter
375 g (625 mℓ/2½ cups) mealie meal

Pour the water into a potjie, add the salt and butter and bring to the boil over hot coals. Pour in the mealie meal to form a cone in the centre of the pot but do not stir. Reduce the heat by removing some coals, cover the potjie and let the pap simmer for 5 minutes. Stir gently with a fork, then cover again and simmer for another hour.
Serves 6

VARIATIONS
Stywepap snacks: When the pap is cooked shape it into balls and roll them in beaten egg and then in herb or Parmesan flavoured breadcrumbs. Fry the balls in hot cooking oil until they are golden brown, drain and serve as a snack.

Alternatively, mould some cooked pap round a cube of cheese and wrap a strip of bacon around it. Secure with a toothpick and braai over hot coals until the bacon is crisp. Serve these, too, as a snack.

Melkpap

500 mℓ (2 cups) milk
500 mℓ (2 cups) water
10 mℓ (2 teaspoons) salt
300 g (500 mℓ/2 cups) mealie meal
2 eggs, beaten
200 g Cheddar cheese, grated (500 mℓ)

Bring the milk, water and salt to the boil in a potjie over hot coals. Pour in the mealie meal to form a cone in the centre of the potjie but resist the temptation to stir. Reduce the heat by removing coals, put the lid on the potjie and let the pap simmer for 5 minutes, until a skin forms. Stir gently, then let it simmer for another hour. After 30 minutes add the eggs and cheese, stirring them in thoroughly.
Serves 10

HINT
The secret of making pap successfully is to let it simmer undisturbed until it is smooth.

Mieliepaptert

1 recipe Stywepap (opposite page)
250 g bacon, finely chopped
300 g mushrooms, chopped
125 ml (½ cup) cream or evaporated milk
100 g Cheddar cheese, grated (250 ml)
1 x 410 g can whole kernel sweetcorn
    (optional)
freshly ground black pepper to taste
extra grated cheese to garnish

Make the Stywepap, spoon it into a greased loaf pan and let it cool and set. In a heavy-based saucepan fry the bacon in its own fat until it is crisp. Add the mushrooms and fry them gently, then stir in the cream, cheese, sweetcorn and pepper. Turn the pap out of the loaf pan and cut it horizontally into 2 or 4 uniformly thick pieces. In a suitable dish, arrange the pap and mushroom filling in layers, ending with the filling, and sprinkle extra cheese over. Cover and braai on a grid over moderate coals for about 30 minutes, or bake at 170 °C for 30 minutes.
Serves 8

VARIATION
A thin white sauce can be used instead of the cream.

Wine sauce

15 ml (1 tablespoon) cooking oil
1 onion, chopped
1 green pepper, chopped
2 tomatoes, peeled and chopped
1 x 266 g can tomato purée
20 ml (1½ tablespoons) Worcestershire
    sauce
1 ml (a dash) grated nutmeg
20 ml (1½ tablespoons) brown sugar
5 ml (1 teaspoon) salt
freshly ground black pepper to taste
125 ml (½ cup) dry red wine
50 ml (3 tablespoons) port or sherry

Heat the cooking oil in a small potjie and fry the onion and green pepper until the onion is translucent. Add the tomatoes, tomato purée, Worcestershire sauce, nutmeg, sugar and seasoning. Bring to the boil, simmer for 5 minutes, then add the wine and port. Serve hot with pap.
Serves 6 - 8

Banana and onion sauce

30 ml (2 tablespoons) butter
3 onions, chopped
500 ml (2 cups) boiling water
5 ml (1 teaspoon) curry powder
30 ml (2 tablespoons) brown sugar
5 ml (1 teaspoon) dry mustard
30 ml (2 tablespoons) cake flour
5 ml (1 teaspoon) salt
freshly ground black pepper
    to taste
125 ml (½ cup) vinegar
6 bananas, sliced

Melt the butter in a small potjie and fry the onion gently until it is translucent. Add the boiling water and let it simmer for about 3 minutes. Mix together the dry ingredients and the vinegar and stir gradually into the simmering water. Let the sauce cook for another 3 minutes, then set it aside to cool. Add the bananas just before serving the sauce with pap.
Serves 6 - 8

Tomato sauce

30 ml (2 tablespoons) cooking oil
2 onions, sliced
1 green pepper, finely
    chopped
6 tomatoes, peeled and coarsely
    chopped
1 x 410 g can tomato purée
125 ml (½ cup) dry white wine
10 ml (2 teaspoons) Worcestershire
    sauce
10 ml (2 teaspoons) freshly chopped
    herbs (oregano, parsley) or 3 ml
    (a pinch) dried mixed herbs
10 ml (2 teaspoons) brown sugar
5 ml (1 teaspoon) salt
freshly ground black pepper to taste

Heat the cooking oil in a small potjie over hot coals. Fry the onion and green pepper gently until the onion is translucent. Add the remaining ingredients and let the sauce simmer for about 15 minutes. Serve hot with pap.
Serves 8

Mieliepaptert (left) and Melkpap, with Banana and onion sauce

Clockwise from top right: Mustard sauce, Tartare sauce and Jiffy mustard sauce

SAUCES & BUTTERS

Sauces add flavour, colour and a particular character to any dish and can be used very effectively with braaied foods — as long as care is taken that the flavour of the sauce complements rather than overpowers the flavour of the food it is accompanying. Butters, too, can enhance meat, poultry and especially fish with a subtle hint of lemon or herbs, mustard or onion.

A comment at the end of each of the following recipes suggests which foods would benefit most from the sauce or butter in question. All the sauces given can be made in advance and stored.

Tomato sauce

15 mℓ (1 tablespoon) cooking oil
3 onions, finely chopped
2 cloves garlic, finely chopped
1 kg ripe tomatoes, peeled and finely
  chopped
15 mℓ (1 tablespoon) lemon juice
15 mℓ (1 tablespoon) brown sugar
15 mℓ (1 tablespoon) freshly chopped or
  5 mℓ (1 teaspoon) dried basil
salt and freshly ground black pepper

Heat the cooking oil in a pan and fry the onion and garlic until the onion is translucent. Add the remaining ingredients and simmer for 15 minutes.
Complements beef, lamb, chicken and fish.
Makes 500 mℓ

Basic braai sauce

100 mℓ (6 tablespoons) olive oil or
  cooking oil
1 onion, sliced
1 clove garlic, crushed
250 mℓ (1 cup) tomato purée
125 mℓ (½ cup) lemon juice or vinegar

Heat the oil in a small potjie and fry the onion and garlic gently until the onion is translucent. Add the tomato purée and lemon juice and simmer for 15 minutes.
Complements beef, lamb and pork.
Makes 500 mℓ

VARIATIONS
To give extra flavour add: a dash of Worcestershire sauce, Tabasco or chilli sauce; a pinch of cayenne pepper, 10 mℓ (2 teaspoons) French mustard or 10 mℓ (2 teaspoons) soy sauce; 30 mℓ (2 tablespoons) brown sugar.
Monkeygland sauce: Add 60 mℓ (¼ cup) Worcestershire sauce, 15 mℓ (1 tablespoon) chutney and 5 mℓ (1 teaspoon) dry mustard to the Basic braai sauce and mix well.

Jiffy mustard sauce

60 mℓ (¼ cup) prepared mustard
30 mℓ (2 tablespoons) brandy
125 mℓ (½ cup) natural yoghurt
125 mℓ (½ cup) mayonnaise
salt to taste

Mix together all the ingredients.
Complements beef, chicken, venison, pork and smoked pork.
Makes about 350 mℓ

Mustard sauce

30 mℓ (2 tablespoons) dry mustard
200 mℓ (¾ cup) sugar
30 mℓ (2 tablespoons) cornflour
3 mℓ (a pinch) salt
white pepper to taste
2 eggs, beaten
200 mℓ (¾ cup) vinegar

Place the top of a double boiler over simmering water and pour into it all the ingredients except the vinegar, stirring well. Add the vinegar gradually, stirring all the time, and cook until the sauce is thick.
Complements beef, chicken, pork, smoked pork, venison, fish, vegetables and salads.
Makes 400 mℓ

VARIATIONS
To give a herby flavour, add 15 mℓ (1 tablespoon) freshly chopped herbs (oregano, parsley) or 5 mℓ (1 teaspoon) dried mixed herbs. Alternatively, reduce the dry mustard to 20 mℓ (1½ tablespoons) and add 15 mℓ (1 tablespoon) Pommery mustard when the sauce is cooked.

Clockwise from top right: Basic braai sauce, Tomato sauce and Mushroom sauce

Tartare sauce

250 mℓ (1 cup) mayonnaise
3 medium gherkins, chopped
2 spring onions, chopped
1 clove garlic, chopped
30 mℓ (2 tablespoons) freshly chopped
    parsley
15 mℓ (1 tablespoon) chopped green
    pepper
5 mℓ (1 teaspoon) French mustard
10 mℓ (2 teaspoons) lemon juice
freshly ground black pepper to taste

Mix together all the ingredients thoroughly. Place in an airtight container and store in the refrigerator.
Complements fish and salads.
Makes 250 mℓ

Mushroom sauce

70 g (5 tablespoons) butter
200 g mushrooms, sliced
50 mℓ (3 tablespoons) cake flour
250 mℓ (1 cup) milk, heated
250 mℓ (1 cup) chicken stock, heated
salt, freshly ground white pepper and
    grated nutmeg to taste

Melt the butter and fry the mushrooms for a few minutes. Add the cake flour and fry gently, stirring, for 1 minute longer. Pour in the milk and chicken stock and bring to the boil, then reduce the heat and cook gently until the sauce has thickened. Season with salt, pepper and nutmeg.
Complements beef, lamb, venison, chicken and fish.
Makes 500 mℓ

Sweet and sour sauce

1 x 410 g can pineapple chunks, drained
    and liquid reserved
2 cooking apples, peeled and grated
1 green pepper, cut into chunks
30 mℓ (2 tablespoons) cornflour
30 mℓ (2 tablespoons) vinegar
100 mℓ (6 tablespoons) dry white wine
15 mℓ (1 tablespoon) soy sauce
salt and freshly ground black pepper

Let the pineapple chunks, apple and green pepper simmer in the liquid from the canned pineapple for 5 minutes. Mix together the cornflour and the vinegar and add to the mixture with the remaining ingredients. Stir well and simmer for 10 minutes.
Complements beef, pork and chicken.
Makes 375 mℓ

VARIATION
Substitute 1 x 410 g can litchies for the pineapple chunks.

Pepper sauce

50 mℓ (3 tablespoons) butter
1 small onion, finely chopped
50 mℓ (3 tablespoons) green peppercorns,
    slightly crushed
5 mℓ (1 teaspoon) prepared mustard
30 mℓ (2 tablespoons) brandy
250 mℓ (1 cup) cream
30 mℓ (2 tablespoons) freshly chopped
    parsley
3 mℓ (a pinch) salt

Melt the butter and fry the onion until it is translucent. Add the peppercorns and mustard. Warm the brandy in a small container, ignite it and pour it over the onion and peppercorn mixture. Boil the sauce rapidly until it is reduced to one third. Lower the heat, add the cream, parsley and salt and simmer until the sauce is thick.
Complements beef, pork and veal.
Makes 250 mℓ

Back to front: Fruit sauce, Pawpaw purée, Fruity mustard and Prune sauce

Fruity mustard

125 g dried apricots
125 g dried apple rings
750 mℓ (3 cups) water
30 mℓ (2 tablespoons) dry mustard
50 mℓ (3 tablespoons) sherry
10 mℓ (2 teaspoons) wine vinegar
1 mℓ (a dash) ground ginger

Cook the apricots and apple rings in the water until they are soft, then boil rapidly without a lid until the liquid is reduced to about 200 mℓ (¾ cup). Liquidise the fruit and water in a blender, then add the remaining ingredients and mix thoroughly. Store in a sterilised container in the refrigerator.
Complements beef, pork, chicken and lamb.
Makes 500 mℓ

Piquant wine sauce

30 mℓ (2 tablespoons) cooking oil
1 onion, finely chopped
1 clove garlic, crushed
250 mℓ (1 cup) dry white wine
3 mℓ (a pinch) salt
1 mℓ (a dash) dry mustard
30 mℓ (2 tablespoons) tomato sauce
1 mℓ (a dash) Tabasco

Heat the cooking oil and fry the onion and garlic until the onion is translucent. Add the remaining ingredients and simmer for 20 minutes.
Complements beef, lamb, pork and chicken.
Makes 250 mℓ

Fruit sauce

125 mℓ (½ cup) vinegar
125 mℓ (½ cup) brown sugar
50 mℓ (3 tablespoons) prepared mustard
1 x 820 g can tart apples
1 x 820 g can apricots
125 mℓ (½ cup) sultanas

Heat together the vinegar, brown sugar and mustard, stirring until the sugar has dissolved. Add the apples, apricots and sultanas and simmer for 5 minutes.
Complements pork and any kind of smoked meat.
Makes 1 litre

Pawpaw purée

1 small pawpaw
15 mℓ (1 tablespoon) chopped fresh mint
5 mℓ (1 teaspoon) lemon juice
5 mℓ (1 teaspoon) sugar
1 mℓ (a dash) salt

Liquidise all the ingredients in a blender. Chill before serving.
Complements pork and lamb.
Makes 250 mℓ

Prune sauce

10 mℓ (2 tablespoons) cooking oil
2 onions, chopped
50 mℓ (3 tablespoons) honey
125 g stoned prunes, chopped
125 mℓ (½ cup) meat stock
salt and freshly ground black pepper
   to taste

Heat the cooking oil and fry the onions until they are translucent. Add the remaining ingredients and simmer for 2 - 3 minutes.
Complements beef and pork.
Makes 250 mℓ

Savoury butters

Savoury butters are easy to prepare and one method suffices for all the following recipes.

Stir the butter rapidly with a wooden spoon to soften it. Season with the appropriate flavouring and mix thoroughly. On a piece of foil or cling wrap, shape the butter into a roll, wrap it and freeze it. Use within 2 weeks. Serve thick slices of the butter on hot food.

Ginger butter

125 g (½ cup) butter
10 mℓ (2 teaspoons) chopped root ginger
salt and freshly ground black pepper

Complements pork and lamb.

Garlic butter

125 g (½ cup) butter
3 cloves garlic, chopped
salt to taste

Complements beef, lamb, pork, chicken, fish and vegetables.

Tabasco butter

125 g (½ cup) butter
5 mℓ (1 teaspoon) Tabasco
salt and freshly ground black pepper
   to taste

Complements pork.

Mint butter

125 g (½ cup) butter
15 mℓ (1 tablespoon) chopped fresh mint

Complements lamb and tunny.

Parsley butter

125 g (½ cup) butter
10 mℓ (2 teaspoons) chopped parsley
10 mℓ (2 teaspoons) lemon juice

Complements lamb, chicken, fish and vegetables.

Left to right: Tabasco butter, Mustard butter, Garlic butter, Mixed herb butter and Mint butter

Mustard butter

125 g (½ cup) butter
5 mℓ (1 teaspoon) dry mustard or 10 mℓ
   (2 teaspoons) prepared mustard
salt to taste

Complements beef, lamb, pork, sausages and hamburgers.

Mixed herb butter

125 g (½ cup) butter
10 mℓ (2 teaspoons) chopped onion
60 mℓ (¼ cup) freshly chopped herbs
   (rosemary, thyme, marjoram, oregano)
   or 20 mℓ (1½ tablespoons) dried mixed
   herbs
10 mℓ (2 teaspoons) lemon juice

Complements beef, lamb, pork, chicken and fish.

Lemon butter

125 g (½ cup) butter
10 mℓ (2 teaspoons) lemon juice
2 cloves garlic, crushed
salt and freshly ground black pepper
   to taste

Complements white fish, chicken and beef.

Onion butter

125 g (½ cup) butter
30 mℓ (2 tablespoons) chopped onion
10 mℓ (2 teaspoons) freshly chopped
   parsley
salt to taste

Complements vegetables, beef, lamb and pork.

Clockwise from top right: Apple drink, Fruit refresher and Kids' punch

DRINKS & DESSERTS

Ice-cold beer, wine, cooldrink and fresh fruit juices all go down well at any braai, but you can add extra sparkle by serving a special blend of your own — ice-cold, of course. And, for a finishing touch, treat your family and friends to a delicious dessert cooked over the last embers of the fire — or, if the evening is becoming chill, to a warming, liquor-laced coffee.

Kids' punch

1 x 80 g packet lime jelly (or any other flavour)
375 mℓ (1½ cups) boiling water
750 mℓ (3 cups) ginger beer
ice cubes
mint leaves to garnish

In a large jug, dissolve the jelly powder in the boiling water, add the ginger beer and chill. Pour over ice cubes in a glass and decorate with mint leaves.
Makes about 1 litre

Fruit refresher

12 bananas
1 pawpaw, peeled and roughly chopped
1 pineapple, peeled and roughly chopped
750 mℓ (3 cups) sugar
1 x 60 g packet tartaric acid
6 litres water
2 x 110 g cans granadilla pulp
1 x 750 mℓ bottle lemon squash
1 x 750 mℓ bottle orange squash
1 litre (4 cups) apricot juice

Place the fruit in a blender and liquidise, or chop as finely as you can. Dissolve the sugar and tartaric acid in the water and add to the fruit, together with the remaining ingredients. Mix well and chill.
Makes 10 litres

HINT
Make a refreshing drink by mixing 2 parts chilled rooibos tea with 1 part orange juice and 1 part pineapple juice.

Apple drink

375 mℓ (1½ cups) apple juice
125 mℓ (½ cup) orange juice
125 mℓ (½ cup) pineapple juice
50 mℓ (3 tablespoons) boiling water
15 mℓ (1 tablespoon) freshly chopped mint

Pour the fruit juices into a large jug and stir. Pour boiling water over the mint and allow to stand for 15 minutes. Strain and add the liquid to the fruit juices. Chill well.
Makes 650 mℓ

Sangria

2 x 750 mℓ bottles dry red wine
60 mℓ (¼ cup) brandy
30 mℓ (2 tablespoons) lemon juice
60 mℓ (¼ cup) brown sugar
1 orange, sliced thinly
1 lemon, sliced thinly
375 mℓ (1½ cups) soda water, chilled
crushed ice

Pour the wine, brandy and lemon juice into
a large jug and add the brown sugar, stirring until it has dissolved. Add the orange
and lemon slices, then pour in the chilled
soda water just before serving. Serve in tall
glasses over crushed ice.
Makes 2 litres

Braai punch

250 mℓ (1 cup) sugar
750 mℓ (3 cups) water
juice of 6 oranges (about 625 mℓ/2½ cups)
juice of 6 lemons (about 250 mℓ/1 cup)
2 - 3 bananas, sliced thinly
1 x 410 g can pineapple chunks
125 mℓ (½ cup) fresh or canned cherries,
    stoned and halved
2 x 110 g cans granadilla pulp
2 litres ginger ale
1 x 750 mℓ bottle semi-sweet white wine

Pour the sugar and water into a large jug
and stir briskly to dissolve the sugar. Add
the remaining ingredients and chill well.
Makes 5 litres

Grapefruit drink

625 mℓ (2½ cups) grapefruit juice
20 mℓ (1½ tablespoons) lemon juice
625 mℓ (2½ cups) ginger ale, chilled
lemon slices and sprigs of mint to
    garnish

Pour the grapefruit juice and lemon juice
into a large jug, stir and chill well. Add the
ginger ale just before serving. Garnish with
lemon slices and sprigs of mint.
Makes 1,25 litres

*Clockwise from top right: Grapefruit drink, Braai
punch and Sangria*

Chocolate fondue (back) and Pancakes

On a hot day ice-cream is very welcome at a braai. To make your own, chill a 410 g can evaporated milk. Whisk the milk until it is thick, at the same time pouring in a 397 g can condensed milk. Add a 90 g packet instant pudding (any flavour) and whisk again. Freeze, then store in the freezer until required. Serve with Chocolate or Caramel sauce (see Chocolate fondue, below left).

Pancakes

120 g (250 mℓ/1 cup) cake flour
5 mℓ (1 teaspoon) baking powder
2 mℓ (a pinch) salt
2 eggs
200 mℓ (¾ cup) milk
200 mℓ (¾ cup) water
5 mℓ (1 teaspoon) brandy or lemon juice
125 mℓ (½ cup) cooking oil
lemon slices to garnish

VAN DER HUM SAUCE
60 mℓ (¼ cup) Van der Hum liqueur
120 g (½ cup) butter
250 mℓ (1 cup) brown sugar
3 mℓ (a pinch) ground cinnamon
3 mℓ (a pinch) grated lemon rind
4 bananas, halved lengthwise

Sift together the flour, baking powder and salt. Beat together the eggs and milk and stir into the flour mixture. Add the water and beat the mixture until it has the consistency of thin cream. Pour in the brandy and cooking oil and stir thoroughly. Cook the pancakes in a greased, heavy-based frying pan over hot coals. To make the sauce, heat together the Van der Hum, butter, brown sugar, cinnamon and lemon rind, stirring until the butter has melted and the sugar dissolved. Add the bananas and simmer for a few minutes. Place a banana half on each pancake and roll up. Place in a serving dish and pour the remaining sauce over. Serve each pancake with a slice of lemon.
Makes 12 - 15 pancakes

Chocolate fondue

Provide any of the following dippers:
• **fruit (grapes, litchis, strawberries, paw-paw cubes, banana chunks, prunes, orange slices, melon balls, pear cubes)**
• **marshmallows**
• **sponge fingers or sweet biscuits**
• **cubes of fruit cake or sponge cake**

CHOCOLATE SAUCE
100 g milk chocolate, broken into small
    pieces
50 mℓ (3 tablespoons) cream
5 - 10 mℓ (1 - 2 teaspoons) Van der Hum
    liqueur, brandy or rum

Prepare the sauce in advance and warm it gently in a potjie over low coals when you are ready for the dessert. To make the sauce, heat together the chocolate and cream, stirring frequently. Remove from the heat and stir in the Van der Hum, brandy or rum. Prepare the fruit if necessary and arrange the dippers attractively, allowing 125 - 250 mℓ (½ - 1 cup) fruit and 4 - 6 bite-sized portions of cake per person.
Makes 250 mℓ sauce

VARIATION
Caramel sauce: Melt 150 g cream caramel toffees very slowly, stirring constantly until the mixture is smooth. Add 125 mℓ (½ cup) cream and 30 mℓ (2 tablespoons) butter and stir until the butter has melted.

┌─*HINT*─────────────────────
Fruit such as pineapple chunks, strawberries, kiwi fruit chunks and cherries can be threaded onto thin kebab skewers and then dipped into the sauce.
└───────────────────────────

┌─*HINT*─────────────────────
The pancakes will turn out better if you make the batter 1 hour before cooking and refrigerate it.
└───────────────────────────

Baked pineapple

2 small pineapples
125 mℓ (½ cup) brown sugar
60 g (¼ cup) butter
125 mℓ (½ cup) brandy
5 mℓ (1 teaspoon) ground cinnamon

Cut a thick slice from the side of each pine-apple and scoop out balls of flesh. Toss the pineapple balls in the brown sugar and re-place in the shells. Dot each with butter and sprinkle the brandy and cinnamon over. Replace the slices on the pineapples and wrap each securely in heavy foil. Braai over moderate coals for about 10 minutes on each side. Just before serving, open up the foil and remove the pineapple lids. Serve hot.
Serves 2

To ensure that your potjie is clean before you start cooking in it, boil some water in it while the fire is hot.

Bananas with cream cheese

30 mℓ (2 tablespoons) butter
6 bananas, sliced
125 mℓ (½ cup) cream cheese
75 mℓ (5 tablespoons) brown sugar
5 mℓ (1 teaspoon) ground cinnamon
30 mℓ (2 tablespoons) brandy
cream to serve

Melt the butter on a skottel braai and fry the bananas slightly. Mix together the cream cheese, brown sugar, cinnamon and bran-dy. Spoon the bananas into a greased foil pie dish and pour the cream cheese mixture over. Cover with foil and bake over low coals for 15 - 20 minutes. Serve with cream.
Serves 4

VARIATIONS
Bananas in foil: Wrap a peeled banana, 3 marshmallows and half a chocolate Flake in foil. Cook among moderate coals for about 15 minutes.

Alternatively, slice 1 banana onto the shiny side of a piece of foil, sprinkle 15 mℓ (1 tablespoon) brown sugar, 5 mℓ (1 tea-spoon) ground cinnamon and 5 mℓ (1 tea-spoon) lemon juice over. Wrap and cook among moderate coals for about 15 minutes.

Back to front: Baked pineapple, Apple packets and Bananas with cream cheese

Apple packets

6 small apples, peeled, cored and sliced
125 mℓ (½ cup) seedless raisins
3 mℓ (a pinch) ground cinnamon
3 mℓ (a pinch) grated nutmeg
50 mℓ (3 tablespoons) lemon juice
125 mℓ (½ cup) golden syrup or honey
60 mℓ (¼ cup) brown sugar
60 g (125 mℓ/½ cup) cake flour
salt to taste
80 g (5 tablespoons) butter
80 g Cheddar cheese, grated (200 mℓ)

Divide the apple slices and raisins into 6 equal portions and place a portion of each on a greased square of foil. Sprinkle cinna-mon, nutmeg and lemon juice over each portion and spoon the golden syrup on top. Mix together the sugar, cake flour and salt, and rub the butter into the dry ingredients with your fingertips. Add the cheese and sprinkle the mixture over the apples. Wrap the foil securely around the apples and cook on a grid over low coals for 12 - 15 min-utes, turning frequently.
Serves 6

VARIATIONS
Other fruits, such as bananas, oranges, peaches, pears and pineapple, can also be cooked in foil. Peel the fruit and slice or keep whole. Flavour it with sugar and but-ter and sprinkle cinnamon over apples and oranges. Wrap the fruit securely in foil and cook on a grid or among low coals, turning once or twice. Use a fork to pierce the foil and test whether the fruit is cooked.

Back to front: Crumpets, Potjie dumplings and Welbeloontjies

Potjie dumplings

120 g (½ cup) butter
60 mℓ (¼ cup) smooth apricot jam
15 mℓ (1 tablespoon) bicarbonate of soda
240 g (500 mℓ/2 cups) cake flour, sifted
2 mℓ (a pinch) salt
125 mℓ (½ cup) milk

HANEPOOT SAUCE
500 mℓ (2 cups) water
200 mℓ (¾ cup) hanepoot wine
200 mℓ (¾ cup) brown sugar
10 mℓ (2 teaspoons) butter
1 mℓ (a dash) ground ginger
1 mℓ (a dash) ground cinnamon
1 mℓ (a dash) ground cloves

Melt the butter in a saucepan and add the jam and then the bicarbonate of soda. Remove from the heat and stir in the sifted cake flour and salt. Pour in the milk and mix thoroughly to a smooth batter. To make the sauce, put all the ingredients in a potjie and bring to the boil over hot coals. Simmer for a few minutes until the sugar has dissolved, then drop spoonfuls of the batter into the simmering liquid. Cover with the lid and simmer over low coals for 25 minutes without removing the lid.
Serves 6

┌─**HINT**────────────────────
For this and other dessert recipes that include a batter or dough, you may find it easier to prepare the batter beforehand in the kitchen.
└──────────────────────────

Welbeloontjies

240 g (500 mℓ/2 cups) cake flour
10 mℓ (2 teaspoons) baking powder
10 mℓ (2 teaspoons) sugar
2 mℓ (a pinch) salt
30 mℓ (2 tablespoons) butter
1 egg, beaten
75 mℓ (5 tablespoons) milk
75 mℓ (5 tablespoons) water
apricot jam, honey or golden syrup

Sift together the flour, baking powder, sugar and salt. Rub the butter into the dry ingredients with your fingertips. Add the egg, milk and water and mix to a firm dough. Roll the dough out thinly and cut into strips 20 mm wide and 350 mm long. Cover with a moist cloth until required. Choose 6 sticks, each about 500 mm long and 15 mm thick, and remove the bark about 120 mm from one end. Wrap a strip of dough around the debarked end of the stick, moistening and sealing together the overlapping edges. Braai over moderate coals, turning the stick frequently, until the pastry is light brown and cooked. Slip the welbeloontjie off the stick, spoon jam, honey or syrup into the hole and serve immediately.
Serves 6

┌─**HINT**────────────────────
Choose poplar sticks if you can, but on no account select sticks from an oleander bush – it is poisonous.
└──────────────────────────

Crumpets

240 g (500 mℓ/2 cups) cake flour
30 mℓ (2 tablespoons) baking powder
10 mℓ (2 teaspoons) salt
30 mℓ (2 tablespoons) sugar
1 egg
500 mℓ (2 cups) milk
30 mℓ (2 tablespoons) cooking oil
butter, syrup or honey to serve

Sift together the flour, baking powder and salt and add the sugar. Beat the egg, milk and cooking oil, pour into the flour and mix to a thin batter. Heat a greased baking sheet over moderate coals, drop spoonfuls of the batter onto the sheet and cook until golden brown. Serve with butter, syrup or honey.
Makes 30

Fruit salad

1 pawpaw or spanspek, scooped into
   balls
150 g grapes, pips removed
2 green apples, cut into wedges and
   sprinkled with lemon juice
250 g stewed or canned cling peaches
250 g stewed fresh plums or prunes
1 pineapple, sliced
sprigs of mint to garnish

SYRUP
125 mℓ (½ cup) sugar
125 mℓ (½ cup) water
125 mℓ (½ cup) port
1 stick cinnamon
2 mℓ (½ teaspoon) vanilla essence
a piece of lemon rind

Prepare the syrup by heating all the ingredients very slowly in a potjie over low coals
until the sugar has dissolved completely.
Bring to the boil, add the peaches and
plums and simmer for 5 minutes. Allow to
cool in the syrup. Arrange the fruits in layers in a glass bowl and pour the syrup over.
Garnish with sprigs of mint.
Serves 12

VARIATION
Use 750 g mixed dried fruit instead of the
fresh fruit and let it simmer in the syrup for
10 minutes.

┌─*HINT*──────────────────────┐
Fruit steeped in white, red or any fortified
wine and served with whipped cream makes
a refreshing dessert.
└──────────────────────────┘

Clockwise from top right: Irish coffee, Fruit salad and Kahlua pedro

Irish coffee

30 mℓ (2 tablespoons) brown sugar
150 mℓ (10 tablespoons) whisky
1,2 litres (5 cups) strong coffee
200 mℓ (¾ cup) cream, whipped

Spoon 5 mℓ (1 teaspoon) sugar and 25 mℓ
(2 tablespoons) whisky into each of 6 Irish
coffee glasses and stir gently. Add piping
hot coffee and stir again. Pour cream over
the back of a spoon onto the coffee and
serve immediately.
Serves 6

VARIATIONS
Experiment with brandy or any liqueur of
your choice instead of the whisky.

Kahlua pedro

750 mℓ (3 cups) vanilla ice-cream
125 mℓ (½ cup) fresh cream
125 mℓ (½ cup) milk
125 mℓ (½ cup) Kahlua or any other coffee
   liqueur
50 g Peppermint Crisp, grated

Let the ice-cream stand at room temperature to soften slightly. Beat together the
ice-cream, fresh cream and milk, add the
Kahlua and mix well. Pour into glasses and
sprinkle grated Peppermint Crisp over.
Serves 6

INDEX